ADAPTIVE FASHION HANDBOOK

DIY SOLUTIONS FOR INCLUSIVE STYLE

EMPOWERING PERSONAL STYLE FOR EVERY ABILITY

KASHVI KHURANA

Dedication

This book is dedicated to every individual
who has ever felt unseen by the fashion industry.

To those who have struggled to find clothing that fits both
their body and their identity—this is for you.

To the caregivers who dress their loved ones with patience,
care, and love—this is for you.

To the designers and innovators who believe that fashion
should be for everyone—this is for you.

To anyone who has ever thought, "I wish dressing up was
easier, more stylish, more me."

Know this: You deserve fashion that works for YOU.

This book is a step toward a world where
fashion is truly inclusive—without limits,
without barriers, without compromise.

Contents

Chapter 10: DIY Adaptive Fashion Hacks for Everyday Wear   68

Acknowledgments

This book would not have been possible without the stories, struggles, and victories of those who continue to redefine adaptive fashion every day.

A heartfelt thank you to:

- The individuals and families who shared their experiences—your voices are powerful, and your journeys inspire change.

- The caregivers who make dressing a dignified experience—your patience and love bring confidence to others.

- The designers and tailors creating adaptive clothing—your work is shaping the future of fashion.

- The readers who believe in inclusive fashion— your awareness and support will make adaptive fashion mainstream.

To everyone who dares to challenge outdated norms, who believes that fashion should adapt to people, not the other way around—thank you.

This is only the beginning.

- Would you like to add a note about yourself as the author, or any final message for the reader?

A Personal Note from the Author

As I complete this book, I realize that adaptive fashion is not just about clothing—it's about dignity, confidence, and self-expression.

Every thread, every modification, and every small design choice can change the way a person feels about themselves. Whether you're someone who needs adaptive clothing, a caregiver looking for solutions, or a designer eager to make a difference, I hope this book has opened your eyes to the limitless possibilities of inclusive fashion.

Fashion should never be a barrier. It should be a tool of empowerment, allowing everyone to step out into the world feeling their best, most authentic selves.

This book was written not just to share knowledge but to ignite change. If even one reader walks away feeling more confident in their clothing choices—or a designer decides to make fashion more inclusive—then this journey has been worth it.

In compiling this handbook, I have drawn from years of hands-on experience, real-world case studies, and research. Some sections have been enhanced with digital tools for clarity and accessibility, but every insight and recommendation stems from genuine understanding and lived experience.

Here's to a future where fashion is truly for everyone.

With gratitude and hope,

Kashvi Khurana

Acknowledgements

First and foremost, I would like to express my deepest gratitude to my parents for their unwavering support and encouragement throughout this journey. Their belief in me has been my greatest source of strength.

To my mentors, teachers, and friends, thank you for guiding me, sharing your knowledge, and always pushing me to strive for more. Your advice has been invaluable, and I am truly grateful for the role each of you has played in my life.

A special thank you to the adaptive fashion community, whose creativity and dedication to inclusivity inspired the foundation of this book. Your innovative approaches to solving real-world challenges have sparked a movement that I am proud to contribute to.

I would also like to extend my heartfelt appreciation to the individuals who shared their personal stories with me. Your experiences shaped the narrative of this book and highlighted the real impact that adaptive fashion can have on people's lives.

Finally, to everyone who believes in the power of fashion to transform lives—thank you. This book is for you. Together, we can build a world where fashion is truly inclusive, empowering individuals to express themselves with confidence and comfort.

With love and gratitude,

Kashvi Khurana

Chapter 1

Introduction

Empowering personal style for every ability

Fashion is more than just clothing—it is a reflection of identity, culture, and individuality. However, mainstream fashion often overlooks the needs of individuals with physical, sensory, or mobility challenges. *The Adaptive Fashion Handbook: DIY Solutions for Inclusive Style* is a step toward bridging this gap by offering practical, do-it-yourself (DIY) solutions that make fashion both functional and stylish for all.

Whether you are an individual seeking greater independence, a caregiver looking for adaptive solutions, or a designer interested in inclusive fashion, this book provides the tools, techniques, and inspiration to modify clothing in a way that enhances both comfort and style.

1.1 Defining Adaptive Fashion

Adaptive fashion refers to clothing and accessories specifically designed to meet the unique needs of individuals with physical, sensory, or cognitive challenges. Unlike conventional apparel, adaptive clothing integrates features that enhance accessibility, including:

- **Easy Closures** – Velcro, magnetic snaps, and elastic bands replacing traditional buttons and zippers for effortless dressing.

- **Adjustable Fits** – Elastic waistbands, stretch panels, and adjustable straps to accommodate different body shapes, medical devices, and mobility aids.

- **Seamless & Sensory-Friendly Designs** – Soft fabrics, flat seams, and tag-free clothing to reduce irritation for those with sensory sensitivities.

- **Accessible Openings** – Strategically placed fastenings that simplify dressing for individuals with limited mobility or medical needs.

The purpose of adaptive fashion is to ensure that clothing is not only practical but also empowering, allowing individuals to express their personal style with confidence.

1.2 Importance of Inclusivity in Fashion

Fashion should be a space for self-expression that welcomes all individuals, regardless of their physical abilities. Embracing inclusivity in fashion is essential because:

- **It fosters representation.** When fashion reflects diverse abilities, individuals feel acknowledged and valued.

- **It promotes independence.** Adaptive clothing enhances autonomy by making dressing easier and more manageable.

- **It encourages innovation.** Designing for inclusivity leads to new technologies and materials that benefit a broader audience.

- **It breaks societal barriers.** Prioritizing accessibility in fashion challenges traditional norms, paving the way for a more inclusive world.

Inclusivity in fashion is not a trend—it is a necessary step toward equality and dignity for all individuals.

1.3 Why DIY: Empowering Through Customization

Many adaptive fashion solutions available in the market are expensive, difficult to source, or lack personalization. DIY adaptive fashion provides an alternative by allowing individuals to modify their clothing according to their unique preferences and needs.

- **Personalization:** DIY techniques allow for complete control over fit, comfort, and style.

- **Affordability:** Modifying existing garments is often more cost-effective than purchasing specialized adaptive clothing.

- **Skill Development:** Learning to adapt clothing fosters creativity, problem-solving, and valuable sewing skills.

- **Community Building:** Engaging in DIY adaptive fashion creates a network of like-minded individuals who share ideas and solutions.

By embracing DIY adaptive fashion, individuals can take charge of their wardrobe, ensuring that clothing is both functional and expressive of their personal identity.

Chapter 2

Understanding Adaptive Fashion Needs

Creating fashion that supports comfort, independence, and inclusivity

Adaptive fashion is not just about modifying clothing—it is about understanding the diverse needs of individuals who face unique challenges in dressing. Whether due to physical limitations, sensory sensitivities, or mobility restrictions, the right clothing modifications can significantly improve comfort, ease of wear, and overall confidence.

2.1 Identifying Physical, Sensory, and Mobility Challenges

Different individuals have different adaptive needs, which fall into three primary categories:

A. Physical Challenges

People with physical conditions may experience difficulty with traditional fastenings, restrictive fits, or dressing independently. Common challenges include:

- **Limited Dexterity** – Conditions such as arthritis, muscular dystrophy, or stroke-related impairments can make buttons, zippers, and small fastenings difficult to manage.

- **Prosthetics & Medical Devices** – Individuals who use prosthetics or medical devices (such as insulin pumps, catheters, or braces) require clothing with adjustable openings or flexible fabrics.

- **Joint Stiffness & Restricted Motion –** Conditions such as cerebral palsy or multiple sclerosis may require wider openings, slip-on styles, or garments that allow ease of movement.

B. Sensory Challenges

For individuals with autism, sensory processing disorders, or hypersensitivity, textures and seams can cause discomfort. Key considerations include:

- **Fabric Sensitivity –** Rough textures, tags, or synthetic materials may feel irritating. Soft, breathable, and seamless fabrics work best.

- **Temperature Regulation Issues –** Some individuals struggle to maintain body temperature and require moisture-wicking, breathable, or thermal fabrics.

- **Noise Sensitivity –** The sound of Velcro or stiff fabrics rubbing together may be uncomfortable for individuals with auditory sensitivities.

C. Mobility Challenges

For individuals with mobility impairments, clothing must be designed for ease of movement and accessibility. Modifications often include:

- **Seated-Position Comfort –** Wheelchair users require longer back panels, non-bunching fabric, and garments without pressure points.

- **Adaptive Fastenings** – Magnetic closures, Velcro strips, and easy-pull zippers replace traditional fasteners for ease of wear.

- **Adjustable Hemlines & Sleeves** – Clothing should be tailored to avoid dragging or interference with assistive devices.

2.2 Common Barriers in Mainstream Clothing

Traditional fashion is often not designed with accessibility in mind. Common challenges include:

- **Inaccessible Fastenings** – Small buttons, tight hooks, and back zippers can be difficult for individuals with limited dexterity.

- **Rigid & Non-Stretchable Fabrics** – Many mainstream garments do not accommodate changing body shapes, medical devices, or ease of movement.

- **Sensory Irritants** – Scratchy tags, rough seams, and synthetic materials can cause discomfort or irritation.

- **Seated Fit Issues** – Clothing designed for standing positions may bunch up uncomfortably when seated.

- **Lack of Representation in Fashion** – The fashion industry often overlooks the need for stylish, functional adaptive wear.

2.3 Benefits of Adaptive and Custom Clothing

Adaptive and DIY-modified clothing offers a range of benefits, improving quality of life through:

- **Increased Independence** – Self-dressing features like elastic waistbands and front closures empower individuals to dress without assistance.

- **Enhanced Comfort** – Soft fabrics, tag-free designs, and flexible fits cater to individual sensitivities and mobility needs.

- **Customization for Medical Needs** – Adaptive designs allow easy access to medical devices, braces, and prosthetics.

- **Boosted Confidence** – Stylish yet functional clothing ensures individuals feel good in what they wear.

- **Greater Social Inclusion** – When fashion accommodates all abilities, individuals can fully participate in professional, social, and cultural activities.

By understanding the specific challenges people face in dressing, adaptive fashion can create practical solutions that prioritize both functionality and personal style.

Chapter 3

Essential Tools and Materials

Building a foundation for DIY adaptive fashion

Creating adaptive clothing requires specific tools and materials to ensure comfort, accessibility, and durability. Whether making simple modifications or designing fully customized garments, having the right resources makes the process smoother and more efficient.

3.1 Basic Sewing and Crafting Tools

To begin modifying garments, a basic sewing kit with adaptive-friendly tools is essential. These tools help make precise adjustments while ensuring the durability of modifications.

- **Measuring Tape** – Ensures accurate sizing and fit adjustments.

- **Fabric Scissors** – Sharp scissors dedicated to fabric cutting prevent fraying.

- **Sewing Needles & Pins** – Various sizes for different fabric thicknesses.

- **Sewing Machine (Optional)** – Increases efficiency and ensures durable stitching.

- **Seam Ripper** – Helps remove stitches for alterations or corrections.

- **Fabric Glue & Fusible Tape** – Ideal for no-sew modifications like hemming and attaching fastenings.

- **Tailor's Chalk or Fabric Markers** – Used for marking alterations and design placements.

- **Iron & Ironing Board** – Helps in pressing seams for a polished finish.

While a sewing machine is beneficial, many adaptive modifications can be made using hand-sewing techniques, fabric glue, or fusible tape.

3.2 Choosing Fabrics for Comfort and Accessibility

The choice of fabric is crucial in adaptive fashion, as it affects comfort, durability, and ease of movement. Key considerations include:

A. Breathability & Comfort

- **Cotton** – Soft, breathable, and hypoallergenic, ideal for everyday wear.

- **Bamboo Fabric** – Moisture-wicking, antibacterial, and gentle on sensitive skin.

- **Modal & Tencel** – Derived from natural fibers, they are soft, flexible, and durable.

B. Stretchability & Flexibility

- **Jersey Knit** – Provides stretch without restricting movement, great for tops and leggings.

- **Spandex/Elastane Blends** – Adds flexibility to clothing, accommodating body movements and medical devices.

C. Sensory-Friendly Options

- **Flannel & Fleece** – Soft, non-irritating materials perfect for cooler climates.

- **Seamless & Tag-Free Fabrics** – Reduces irritation for individuals with sensory sensitivities.

D. Special-Purpose Fabrics

- **Moisture-Wicking Fabrics** – Helps regulate temperature and keeps the skin dry.

- **Anti-Microbial Fabrics** – Useful for individuals with prolonged sitting needs to prevent infections.

Selecting fabrics based on individual needs ensures adaptive clothing is both functional and comfortable.

3.3 Understanding Fastenings: Velcro, Zippers, Magnetic Closures

Fastenings play a crucial role in making garments easier to wear. Choosing the right fastening type can enhance accessibility, especially for individuals with dexterity challenges.

A. Velcro Fastenings

- **Pros:** Easy to open and close, adjustable fit, secure hold.

- **Best For:** Shirts, jackets, pants, and footwear straps.

- **DIY Tip:** Use sew-on Velcro for durability or adhesive Velcro for quick, no-sew modifications.

B. Zippers & Modified Pulls

- **Pros:** Secure, versatile, and available in various styles.

- **Best For:** Jackets, bags, pants, and footwear.

- **DIY Tip:** Attach a fabric loop or keyring to the zipper pull for easier grip.

C. Magnetic Closures

- **Pros:** Effortless fastening, ideal for individuals with severe mobility challenges.

- **Best For:** Jackets, shirts, and adaptive accessories.

- **DIY Tip:** Use lightweight magnetic snaps for shirts and heavier-duty ones for coats.

Fastening modifications are among the simplest ways to make clothing

Chapter 4

Creating Adaptive Fastenings

Fastenings are the backbone of adaptive fashion. The ability to quickly modify closures can make a garment easier to wear, improving both comfort and independence. In this chapter, we will explore different types of adaptive fastenings, their benefits, and step-by-step instructions for integrating them into everyday clothing.

4.1 Modifying Clothes with Velcro, Magnets, and Easy Zippers

Adapting fastenings can significantly reduce the effort required to put on or take off clothing. Velcro, magnets, and modified zippers offer simple yet effective solutions that enhance accessibility.

A. Velcro Fastenings

Why Velcro?

Velcro is durable, easy to use, and requires minimal finger dexterity. It is ideal for individuals with arthritis, limited mobility, or muscle weakness.

Where to Use It:

Shirt openings (replace buttons)

Pants and skirts (replace zippers or hooks)

Footwear straps

Saree petticoat closures

DIY Guide:

Materials: Velcro strips (sew-on or adhesive), fabric glue, needle, and thread.

Steps:

Remove the existing buttons or zippers carefully.

Measure and cut Velcro to the desired length.

Sew or glue one strip on each side of the garment opening, ensuring alignment for a secure fit.

Test the fastening by pressing both strips together firmly.

B. Magnetic Closures

Why Magnets?

Magnetic closures are seamless, discreet, and strong. They provide easy closure for individuals with reduced hand strength or fine motor difficulties.

Where to Use It:

Shirt collars

Jackets and outerwear

Kurta plackets

DIY Guide:

Materials: Magnetic snaps, fabric patches, sewing tools.

Steps:

Mark placement points for the magnets along the garment opening.

Sew or glue small fabric patches to secure each magnet, ensuring they align perfectly when closed.

Test the strength of the magnet to ensure it holds under movement.

C. Easy Zippers (Ring Pulls and Extended Tabs)

Why Zippers?

Zippers are already common, but modified zippers make it easier to grip and pull, catering to individuals with limited hand coordination.

Where to Use It:

Jackets

Bags

Dresses and trousers

DIY Guide:

Materials: Large ring pulls, zipper extenders, pliers.

Steps:

Attach a large ring pull or fabric loop to the zipper head.

Use pliers to secure the attachment.

For added convenience, use double-sided zippers to allow opening from either direction.

4.2 Quick-Access Closures for Everyday Wear

Quick-access fastenings transform daily routines, reducing dependency on assistance.

Snap Closures for Pants and Skirts: Replace traditional hooks with snap buttons, allowing quick fastening.

Elastic Bands for Waistlines: Sew elastic bands into the back of waistlines to ensure stretch and ease.

Hook-and-Eye for Saree Blouses: Replace small hooks with larger eyelets and hooks, reducing fine motor effort.

4.3 Adding Elastic for Flexible Fit

Elastic provides flexibility, comfort, and adaptability. It is useful for creating clothing that adjusts to body changes, making garments more forgiving and easier to wear.

Elastic Necklines and Sleeves: Perfect for kurtas and tops, allowing wider openings and easy pull-on designs.

Elastic Waistbands: Ideal for pants, skirts, and salwars, enabling one-size-fits-all solutions.

DIY Guide:

Materials: Elastic bands (1-2 inches wide), sewing machine, pins.

Steps:

Measure the waist or sleeve opening.

Cut elastic slightly shorter than the opening for a snug fit.

Fold the fabric over the elastic and sew along the edge, creating a casing.

Stretch the elastic as you sew to ensure even gathering.

Chapter 5

Designing for Mobility

Adaptive clothing designed for mobility plays a crucial role in enhancing the comfort and independence of individuals who use wheelchairs or experience limited movement. Mobility-friendly designs take into account the seated position, ease of wear, and the ability to dress with minimal assistance. In this chapter, we will focus on modifying garments to accommodate movement restrictions while ensuring style and practicality.

5.1 Adapting Clothing for Wheelchair Users

Clothing for wheelchair users requires specific modifications to ensure comfort, accessibility, and ease of dressing. Garments should reduce pressure points, prevent bunching, and allow for easy movement.

Key Considerations:

Length Adjustments: Garments often shift when seated, requiring shorter front lengths and longer back panels for coverage.

Seam Placement: Seams should be minimal and strategically placed to avoid skin irritation or discomfort.

Fabric Choice: Use stretchable, breathable fabrics that allow flexibility without restricting movement.

DIY Adaptations:

Back-Panel Extensions for Tops and Kurtas: Extend the back hemline by 3-5 inches for added coverage when seated.

Use soft fabric to avoid chafing.

Open-Back Designs for Ease of Dressing: Create an overlapping back panel secured with Velcro or magnets for easy overhead wear.

This works well for kurtas, blouses, and jackets.

Higher Waistbands for Trousers and Salwars: Raise the waistband at the back to ensure trousers stay in place when seated.

Add elastic panels to ensure a flexible, adjustable fit.

Side Zippers or Magnetic Closures: Replace traditional fly closures with side zippers or magnetic strips to allow easier dressing without standing.

5.2 Adjusting Sleeves, Pant Lengths, and Seams

Mobility-friendly garments often require sleeve and pant length adjustments to prevent fabric from gathering or dragging during movement.

Pant Length Adjustments:

Shorter Front, Longer Back: When seated, pants should be slightly longer in the back while the front remains shorter to avoid excess fabric on the lap.

Tapered or Wide-Leg Options: Tapered designs prevent fabric from catching in wheelchair wheels, while wide-leg pants allow easy movement and dressing.

DIY Guide:

Mark the Pants While Seated: Ask the individual to sit while marking the desired length to ensure an accurate fit.

Hem with Elastic: Insert elastic into the hems for a gathered effect, allowing flexibility without being restrictive.

Adjustable Pant Legs with Snaps or Velcro: Add side snaps or Velcro strips along the pant legs for easy adjustment.

Sleeve Modifications:

Shortened Sleeve Lengths: Shorten sleeves at the front to avoid fabric dragging across tables or laps.

Elastic Cuffs: Add elastic or soft ribbing at the cuffs for sleeves that stay in place but stretch as needed.

5.3 Designing Comfortable Outfits for Restricted Movement

For individuals with restricted movement, comfort is paramount. Clothing should accommodate limited joint mobility and ensure easy dressing.

Adaptive Kurta and Salwar Design:

Front Zippers or Button Plackets: Replace traditional side openings with front zippers for easier dressing.

Expandable Side Panels: Insert expandable panels under the arms or along the sides to allow additional room without compromising style.

DIY Adaptation:

Adding Underarm Gussets: Sew triangular fabric inserts under the sleeves to increase range of motion.

Elastic Waist Salwars: Use full elastic waistbands instead of drawstrings to simplify wear.

Soft Fabrics for Long Wear: Choose soft cotton blends or jersey fabrics that are comfortable for extended periods.

Chapter 6

Adapting Traditional Indian Wear

Indian traditional clothing holds deep cultural significance, but it can sometimes present challenges for individuals with mobility issues, sensory sensitivities, or physical limitations. This chapter explores ways to adapt traditional garments like sarees, salwar kameez, kurtas, and lehengas, blending cultural authenticity with ease of wear.

6.1 Adaptive Sarees: Draping and Fastening Techniques

Sarees, while elegant, can be challenging to drape and secure, especially for individuals with limited mobility or dexterity. Adaptive sarees can reduce the need for complex pleating and wrapping, making them more accessible.

Key Modifications:

Pre-Stitched Sarees: Pre-stitch the pleats and pallu (the loose end) to create a ready-to-wear saree that can be slipped on like a skirt.

Attach the pallu with Velcro or a magnetic clip over the shoulder.

Elasticated Petticoats: Replace drawstring petticoats with elastic waistbands for easy pull-on wear.

Use petticoats with side zippers or snaps for added accessibility.

Velcro or Snap Fasteners: Secure the saree at key points (waist and shoulder) using discreet Velcro patches or magnetic buttons, reducing the need for pins.

DIY Guide:

Materials: Lightweight saree fabric, Velcro strips, elastic, sewing tools.

Steps:

Pre-pleat the saree and stitch along the folds.

Attach Velcro at the shoulder and waist to keep the saree in place.

Test the fit, ensuring ease of movement while maintaining the saree's drape.

6.2 Modified Salwar Kameez and Kurtas for Ease of Use

Salwar kameez and kurtas are popular for their comfort and versatility, but adapting them can enhance accessibility further.

Key Modifications:

Front Zippers or Magnetic Closures: Replace back or side openings with front zippers or magnetic strips to simplify dressing.

Expandable Side Panels: Insert elastic or stretchable fabric along the side seams to allow the garment to expand as needed.

Shortened Kurta Lengths (Front Panels): Shorten the front hem slightly while extending the back for seated individuals to ensure proper coverage.

DIY Guide:

Materials: Cotton or blended fabric, zippers, stretchable panels.

Steps:

Add a zipper along the front placket or use snap closures.

Stitch expandable side panels under the arms or along the hips.

Reinforce seams to ensure durability during regular use.

6.3 Blending Tradition with Comfort

Adaptive modifications can maintain the aesthetic of traditional wear while enhancing comfort. This section highlights design changes that preserve the cultural integrity of garments.

Examples:

Lehenga Skirts with Elastic Waists: Replace hooks with fully elasticated waistbands or adjustable drawstrings for easier wear.

Adaptive Dupattas (Scarves): Attach lightweight snaps at the shoulders to secure dupattas, preventing them from slipping.

Velcro Closures for Blouses: Replace the small hooks on blouses with Velcro or magnetic strips to ease wear, especially for individuals with limited hand coordination.

DIY Guide:

For Dupattas: Stitch small loops at each end of the dupatta and use a brooch or snap to attach them to the kurta.

For Lehengas: Sew soft elastic bands along the waistband, ensuring they can stretch to accommodate size changes.

6.4 Adapting Lehengas, Anarkalis, and Men's Traditional Wear

Lehengas, anarkalis, and men's traditional outfits like sherwanis and kurtas hold a special place in Indian culture, often worn during weddings and festivals. Adapting these garments can ensure that individuals with mobility challenges or sensory sensitivities can still participate comfortably in such events.

A. Adaptive Lehengas and Anarkalis

Lehengas and anarkalis are often elaborate, with intricate fastenings and heavy fabrics. Modifications can preserve their elegance while making them easier to wear.

Key Modifications:

Elastic or Adjustable Waistbands: Replace hook-and–eye or zipper closures with elastic or adjustable waistbands for easier wear.

Use drawstring loops with stoppers for precise size adjustments.

Lighter Fabrics: Choose lighter fabric alternatives like georgette, chiffon, or cotton silk to reduce the garment's overall weight.

Side Openings with Velcro or Snaps: Incorporate discreet side Velcro strips or magnetic snaps along the waistband for quick wear and removal.

Pre-Stitched Anarkalis: Pre-stitch the inner layers of anarkalis, allowing them to slip over the head without needing to tie or button multiple layers.

DIY Guide:

Elasticated Lehenga: Measure the waist and cut elastic slightly shorter than the measurement.

Fold the waistband, insert the elastic, and stitch securely.

Side Velcro Fastenings: Attach Velcro along the inner seam, ensuring it aligns perfectly when worn.

B. Adapting Men's Traditional Wear (Sherwanis, Kurtas, and Pajamas)

Men's traditional clothing can also be adapted for comfort and accessibility without compromising on aesthetics.

Key Modifications:

Sherwani with Front Zippers or Magnetic Closures: Replace the buttoned placket of a sherwani with a hidden zipper or magnetic strip to maintain the look while allowing for easy dressing.

Elastic Pajamas and Churidar: Replace drawstrings with elastic bands for quick wear, ensuring the pants adjust to body changes.

Side Openings for Kurtas: Add zippers along the sides or under the arms to allow for step-in dressing rather than pulling overhead.

Velcro Fastened Dupattas and Stoles: Attach small Velcro patches to dupattas or shawls, ensuring they stay in place during movement.

DIY Guide:

Sherwani Modifications: Mark the centerline of the sherwani's placket and carefully remove the buttons.

Insert a concealed zipper, ensuring the outer layer overlaps for a seamless finish.

Elastic Waist Pajamas: Replace the waistband with elastic, securing it with stretchable thread to ensure comfort and fit.

C. Adaptive Accessories

Accessories play a vital role in traditional Indian attire. Adapting them can further enhance ease of wear.

Belts with Magnetic Clasps: Use magnetic clasps instead of traditional buckles for belts that accompany sherwanis and lehengas.

Lightweight Jewelry: Replace heavy necklaces with lightweight alternatives to reduce sensory discomfort.

Simplified Turbans: Pre-tie turbans with Velcro or snap fasteners, allowing quick adjustments without needing to re-tie from scratch.

DIY Guide:

Pre-Tied Turban: Fold and pleat the fabric into the desired turban shape.

Secure the pleats with hidden stitches and add a Velcro strap at the back for adjustable fit.

6.5 Adapting Dupattas, Shawls, and Stoles

Dupattas, shawls, and stoles are integral to Indian attire, but they can often slip, tangle, or become difficult to manage for individuals with limited mobility or sensory sensitivities. Adapting these accessories ensures they remain stylish yet functional.

Key Modifications:

Pre-Attached Dupattas for Lehengas and Salwar Kameez: Stitch one end of the dupatta to the shoulder seam or neckline of the outfit, allowing it to drape naturally without needing constant adjustment.

Loop and Button Attachments: Sew small fabric loops or snap buttons onto the ends of the dupatta and corresponding points on the garment to keep it secured during movement.

Elastic Shoulder Loops: Attach discreet elastic loops on the underside of the garment shoulder, allowing the dupatta to slip through and stay in place.

DIY Guide:

Pre-Attached Dupatta: Pin the dupatta at the desired shoulder point.

Secure with light stitches or Velcro, ensuring the fabric maintains its drape without restricting movement.

Loop and Button Fastenings: Sew loops at the back of the dupatta and attach buttons along the kurta neckline for adjustable fastening.

6.6 Adaptive Bridal and Festive Wear

Bridal and festive attire is often elaborate and multi-layered, which can make dressing independently challenging. Adaptive bridal wear solutions focus on maintaining grandeur while ensuring ease of wear.

Key Modifications:

Two-Piece Lehengas Disguised as One-Piece: Split heavy lehengas into two pieces (skirt and overlay) but stitch them together at the waistband, creating the illusion of a single layered skirt.

Pre-Draped Bridal Dupattas: Instead of carrying multiple dupattas, use a pre-stitched bridal dupatta that can be clipped to the lehenga or blouse at key points.

Open-Back Cholis (Blouses) with Magnetic Closures: Replace back hooks with magnetic strips or Velcro to allow quick dressing without assistance.

Expandable Bridal Attire: Incorporate stretch panels into the sides of blouses and lehengas to allow for size adjustments, accommodating body fluctuations common during long ceremonies.

DIY Guide:

Expandable Choli: Insert soft, stretchable fabric under the arms and along the sides of the blouse.

Sew discreetly beneath the embellishments to maintain design integrity.

Pre-Draped Bridal Dupatta: Pin pleats along one side of the dupatta and attach lightweight hooks to secure it at the waist and shoulder.

6.7 Adapting Festive Wear for Children

Children's festive attire, such as sherwanis, lehengas, and anarkalis, can be adapted to allow more flexibility and easier movement during events.

Key Modifications:

Elastic Inserts in Waistbands: For growing children, add elastic inserts to sherwanis, lehengas, and churidar waistbands for long-term use.

One-Piece Look for Multi-Piece Outfits: Stitch together multi-piece outfits, such as a blouse and lehenga, to prevent the garments from separating during active play.

Snap Closures at Shoulders: Use snap buttons on the shoulders of sherwanis and kurtas to allow easy overhead wear without excessive arm lifting.

DIY Guide:

Elasticated Festive Wear: Sew wide elastic bands into the waistline of churidars or lehengas, ensuring they stretch comfortably.

Snap Closures for Kurtas: Replace the side seams with overlapping fabric panels secured with snap buttons, allowing quick removal.

6.8 Modifying Accessories for Traditional Wear

Accessories like waist belts (kamarbands), anklets, and bangles can sometimes cause discomfort. Adaptive accessories ensure style without sensory discomfort.

Key Modifications:

Adjustable Kamarbands (Waist Belts): Replace metal hooks with elastic or magnetic closures to adjust the fit as needed.

Open Bangles with Hinges: Use hinged bangles that can be opened and closed rather than slipping over the hand.

Soft Anklets: Replace heavy metal anklets with fabric-covered elastic anklets to reduce sensory discomfort.

DIY Guide:

Adjustable Kamarband: Attach elastic strips to both ends of the kamarband and secure with magnetic clasps.

Hinged Bangles: Use bangles with small hinges and clasps that can be easily opened and closed around the wrist.

6.9 Adaptive Traditional Wear for Elders

Elders often face mobility challenges that make traditional clothing difficult to manage. Adapting their attire can preserve dignity and comfort.

Key Modifications:

Velcro-Front Kurtas and Salwar Suits: Replace side openings with full-length Velcro or zipper closures at the front, allowing easy dressing while seated.

Elastic Waist Salwars and Pajamas: Remove drawstrings and replace them with soft elastic to prevent fumbling.

Pre-Stitched Sarees and Lighter Shawls: Provide elders with pre-stitched sarees and lightweight shawls that stay in place with magnetic clips or snap buttons.

DIY Guide:

Pre-Stitched Saree for Elders: Measure the saree to fit the wearer's height. Pre-pleat and stitch the lower half, leaving the pallu free for easy draping.

Elastic Salwar Waistband: Sew elastic into the waist, ensuring gentle stretch and ease of movement.

Chapter 7

Solutions for Sensory Sensitivities

For individuals with sensory sensitivities, the feel of fabric, seams, and tags can cause discomfort or irritation. Adaptive clothing that minimizes these sensory triggers can greatly enhance comfort and quality of life. This chapter focuses on selecting sensory-friendly materials, modifying existing garments, and ensuring a seamless experience for the wearer.

7.1 Sensory – Friendly Fabrics and Textures

The right fabric can make a world of difference for individuals sensitive to touch and texture. Soft, lightweight, and breathable materials help reduce irritation and create a soothing effect.

Key Fabrics to Consider:

Cotton (Organic, Pima, or Brushed): Soft, breathable, and hypoallergenic. Ideal for everyday wear.

Bamboo Fabric: Known for its smooth texture, bamboo fabric is moisture-wicking and gentle on the skin.

Modal and Tencel: Derived from natural fibers, these are soft, durable, and less likely to cause irritation.

Jersey Knit: Stretchy, breathable, and free of harsh seams, jersey knit fabrics work well for undergarments and loungewear.

Flannel and Fleece: Excellent for cooler weather; soft without the bulk of traditional wool.

Fabrics to Avoid: Wool and Rough Linen: These can cause itching and irritation.

Polyester and Nylon: While durable, these synthetic fabrics can trap heat and cause discomfort.

Sequin and Heavy Embellishments: Often scratchy and stiff, these materials can overwhelm individuals with sensory sensitivities.

7.2 Removing Irritating Tags and Seams

Tags and seams are common sources of discomfort. By modifying or eliminating them, clothing can become far more comfortable.

Solutions: Tagless Clothing: Cut out tags and replace them with printed labels. Alternatively, sew soft fabric over the area where tags are removed.

Flat Seams: Re-sew seams to lay flat, reducing friction against the skin. Use techniques like French seams or serging to minimize bulk.

Seamless Garments: For DIY projects, opt for patterns that involve minimal seams or use seamless construction techniques.

Covering Seams with Fabric Tape: Apply soft fabric tape over internal seams to prevent scratching.

DIY Guide:

Removing Tags: Carefully cut the tag close to the seam without damaging the fabric.

If necessary, hand-stitch over the area with soft thread to prevent fraying.

Flattening Seams: Use a zigzag stitch along the seam edge, pressing it flat with an iron for a smooth finish.

7.3 Modifying Waistbands and Cuffs for Comfort

Waistbands and cuffs can feel restrictive and irritating, especially if made from rigid or synthetic materials. Soft, elasticated alternatives provide better comfort without compromising fit.

Key Modifications:

Elastic Waistbands: Use wide elastic bands to replace traditional stiff waistbands. Soft elastics prevent pinching and discomfort.

Drawstrings with Soft Stoppers: Replace hard drawstring closures with fabric or plastic stoppers to reduce sharp edges.

Soft Cuffs: Replace tight cuffs with soft jersey fabric, allowing stretch without digging into the skin.

DIY Guide:

Replacing Waistbands: Remove the existing waistband by carefully unpicking the seams.

Cut soft elastic to the desired length and sew it into the waistband casing.

Soft Cuff Addition: Measure the wrist or ankle opening and cut stretchy fabric to fit.

Sew the fabric to the edge of the sleeve or pant leg, allowing a gentle stretch fit.

7.4 Soft Closures and Fastenings

Zippers, buttons, and metal fasteners can create discomfort through direct contact with sensitive skin. Soft, non-metal alternatives provide functionality while ensuring comfort.

Soft Fastener Options: Magnetic Closures: These eliminate the need for small, difficult-to-use buttons or zippers.

Velcro Strips: Soft Velcro reduces bulk and simplifies fastening without causing skin irritation.

Fabric Ties: Use soft cotton or jersey strips as ties for blouses, pants, or dresses instead of zippers.

Snap Buttons: Plastic snap buttons can be softer and easier to manage than metal fasteners.

DIY Guide:

Replacing Buttons with Velcro: Remove existing buttons and stitch Velcro patches into place.

Ensure the fabric overlaps smoothly to conceal the Velcro when fastened.

Adding Magnetic Closures: Attach small magnetic snaps under the buttonholes of shirts or kurta plackets.

7.5 Breathable Layers for Comfort

Layering can sometimes exacerbate sensory discomfort, especially if the layers are heavy or synthetic. Using soft, breathable inner layers prevents this issue.

Key Modifications: Cotton or Bamboo Linings: Line heavy or embellished garments with cotton or bamboo fabric to create a soft barrier between the skin and the outer layer.

Sleeveless Inner Liners: Use tank tops or slip dresses made of soft jersey under traditional attire.

Breathable Summer Layers: Choose lightweight cotton dupattas or stoles as outer layers instead of synthetic or heavy shawls.

DIY Guide:

Adding Linings: Measure and cut soft fabric to match the garment's inner layer.

Hand-stitch or machine-sew the lining to the inside, ensuring it lays flat.

Chapter 8

Adaptive Fashion for Work and Formal Wear

Dressing for work or formal occasions can be challenging for individuals with limited mobility, dexterity issues, or sensory sensitivities. Adaptive office wear and formal clothing need to balance professionalism, comfort, and accessibility. This chapter explores solutions that ensure style without compromising ease of wear.

8.1 Office Wear with Adaptive Fastenings

Workwear should be practical, stylish, and easy to put on and take off. Small modifications can make blouses, trousers, and suits more accessible while maintaining a professional appearance.

Button-Free Blouses and Shirts: Traditional button-up shirts can be difficult for those with arthritis or hand tremors. Magnetic closures or Velcro strips provide a seamless alternative.

DIY Guide:

Remove existing buttons and stitch magnets or Velcro behind the button placket for an invisible closure.

Ensure strong magnets are used to prevent accidental openings.

Adaptive Trousers and Skirts: Trousers and skirts should allow easy dressing while sitting or standing. Modifications include:

Elastic waistbands to eliminate the need for zippers and buttons.

Side zippers or Velcro panels for step-in dressing.

Pull-on skirts with stretchable fabric to allow independent wear.

Professional Blazers with Adaptive Features: Blazers are a staple in office attire, but their fitted design can make dressing difficult. Modifications such as:

Open-back designs with magnetic closures for easy slip-on wear.

Hidden side zippers to avoid lifting arms overhead.

Stretch panels under the arms for added flexibility.

8.2 Modifications for Corporate and Executive Attire

For those in leadership roles or corporate environments, traditional clothing like sarees, suits, and kurtas need thoughtful adaptations.

Adaptive Sarees for Formal Settings: Pre-stitched sarees or saree gowns provide a professional look without the hassle of draping.

Pre-pleated sarees with an elastic waistband for quick dressing.

Blouses with front zippers or magnetic buttons instead of traditional hooks.

Adjustable pallu fasteners to keep the saree drape secure.

Modified Suits and Sherwanis: For men's formal attire, sherwanis and suits can be adapted with:

Hook-and-loop closures inside suit jackets for effortless dressing.

Stretchable fabric panels in sherwanis to ease movement.

Elastic waist churidars for a tailored look without the need for drawstrings.

Chapter 9

Adaptive Fashion for Travel and Daily Comfort

Traveling or managing day-to-day activities can be exhausting, especially for individuals with mobility challenges, sensory sensitivities, or chronic pain. Adaptive travel clothing should prioritize comfort, ease of wear, and practicality without compromising style. This chapter explores clothing modifications that make travel and everyday dressing stress-free.

9.1 Travel – Friendly Adaptive Clothing

When traveling, clothing should be breathable, wrinkle-free, and easy to put on or remove. The right adaptations can ensure both comfort and independence.

Slip-On Clothing for Easy Dressing: Pull-on pants and skirts: Elastic waistbands eliminate zippers and buttons, making restroom breaks easier.

No-fuss tops: Replace back zippers and buttoned plackets with front closures or wide necklines for easy wear.

Layered outfits with detachable components: Use zip-off sleeves or removable panels for temperature control.

Compression and Support Wear for Long Journeys: For individuals who experience swelling or discomfort during travel, adaptive support wear can provide relief.

Compression leggings and socks improve circulation during long flights or car rides.

Adjustable waistbands prevent tightness or pressure on the abdomen.

Soft, seamless innerwear reduces irritation for sensitive skin.

9.2 Adapting Footwear for Comfort and Accessibility

Shoes should provide both stability and ease of use. Common modifications include:

Velcro or magnetic fasteners instead of laces for quick adjustments.

Stretchable slip-on shoes for swollen feet or orthopedic needs.

Cushioned insoles and non-slip soles for better grip and support.

DIY Guide: Making Shoes More Accessible

Replace regular laces with elastic laces to create slip-on sneakers.

Add memory foam insoles to provide better arch support.

Use heel loops to help pull on shoes without excessive bending.

9.3 Clothing for Daily Comfort and Relaxation

At home, clothing should be breathable, soft, and unrestricted to allow free movement and relaxation.

Adaptive Lounge and Sleepwear: Tag-free, seamless clothing prevents irritation for individuals with sensory sensitivities.

Magnetic or Velcro fastenings in nightwear make dressing effortless.

Temperature-regulating fabrics like bamboo or moisture-wicking cotton help maintain body comfort.

Adaptive Homewear for Elders and Individuals with Limited Mobility

Front-closure nightgowns and kaftans reduce the need for over-the-head dressing.

Side-slit pants with Velcro fastenings make changing easier.

Poncho-style sweaters and shrugs provide warmth without restrictive sleeves.

9.4 Packing Tips for Adaptive Travelers

Packing smartly can make a significant difference for travelers with mobility challenges, sensory sensitivities, or chronic pain. The key is to maximize convenience while minimizing bulk.

Essential Adaptive Travel Clothing Checklist

- Wrinkle-Free Fabrics: Pack breathable materials like bamboo, jersey, or moisture-wicking cotton to avoid ironing.
- Multi-Purpose Clothing: Opt for convertible garments like zip-off pants or jackets with removable sleeves.

- Easy-Fasten Outfits: Prioritize Velcro, magnetic, or elastic closures over buttons and zippers.

- Compression Leggings or Socks: Ideal for long flights or car rides to prevent swelling.

- Slip-On Footwear: Avoid shoes with laces; elasticized or Velcro shoes allow easy wear and removal.

- Lightweight Layering Pieces: Pack ponchos, shawls, or zip-up jackets for temperature fluctuations.

- Pre-Stitched or Adaptive Sarees/Kurtas: If traveling for formal events, pre-stitched sarees and kurtas with front zippers are easy to wear.

Packing Strategies for Accessibility: Use Packing Cubes: Separate daily outfits, innerwear, and essentials to avoid unnecessary digging through a suitcase.

9.5 Seasonal Comfort Clothing

Different seasons require adaptive modifications to enhance comfort while keeping clothing functional.

＊ **Summer Adaptive Wear**

- Moisture-Wicking Fabrics: Lightweight cotton, linen, and bamboo fabrics prevent overheating.

- Loose-Fit Designs: Kaftans, oversized kurtas, and elasticated skirts allow airflow and flexibility.

- Built-in UV Protection: Some modern adaptive fabrics provide sun protection for sensitive skin.

- Easy-Fasten Hats & Scarves: Magnetic closure sun hats and pre-tied scarves offer style with convenience.

❄ **Winter Adaptive Wear**

- Layered Clothing: Zippered cardigans, poncho-style sweaters, and wrap shawls allow easy wear without pulling over the head.

- Thermal Leggings & Soft Wool Socks: Provides warmth without irritation for those sensitive to rough textures.

- Hand Warmer Pockets & Magnetic Mittens: Helps individuals with limited hand mobility stay warm.

- Fleece-Lined Adaptive Coats: Side-zippered jackets ensure easy dressing while keeping the body insulated.

🦗 **Rainy & Monsoon Season Adaptations**

- Waterproof & Quick-Dry Fabrics: Polyester or coated cotton repels water while remaining breathable.

- Slip-Resistant Footwear: Shoes with rubber soles and Velcro closures provide stability.

- Poncho-Style Raincoats: Eliminates the need for sleeve adjustments, making dressing easier.

- Elasticized Hem Pants: Keeps fabric from dragging in puddles or getting caught in wheelchair wheels.

9.6 Layering Tips for Adaptive Dressing

Layering allows for temperature control and comfort, especially for individuals with mobility restrictions, sensory sensitivities, or chronic pain. The key is to use lightweight, breathable, and easy-to-remove layers that adapt to different climates and indoor settings.

Basic Principles of Adaptive Layering

- Prioritize Soft, Stretchable Base Layers – Opt for seamless, moisture-wicking fabrics like cotton, modal, or bamboo for all-day comfort.

- Mid-Layers Should Be Easy to Remove – Use zippers, snap buttons, or magnetic closures instead of pullovers.

- Outer Layers Should Allow Free Movement – Choose poncho-style sweaters, zippered jackets, or wrap shawls instead of restrictive coats.

- Use Temperature-Regulating Accessories – Pre-fastened scarves, wrist warmers, and fleece-lined gloves offer warmth without bulk.

Layering by Season

❈ Summer (Light & Breathable Layers)

Start with a sleeveless cotton tank top as a base layer.

Add a light, oversized linen shirt or open-front kurta for sun protection.

Keep a thin bamboo cardigan or shawl for indoor air-conditioned spaces.

❄ Winter (Warm Yet Flexible Layers)

Base layer: Thermal or fleece-lined cotton top for warmth.

Mid-layer: Poncho or adaptive zip-up sweater for easy removal.

Outer layer: Fleece or waterproof jacket with side zippers for minimal arm movement.

🌴 Rainy Season (Waterproof Yet Comfortable Layers)

Base layer: Quick-dry fabric top (poly-cotton blend) to prevent dampness.

Mid-layer: Thin windbreaker with Velcro fastenings for quick adjustments.

Outer layer: Poncho-style waterproof cape for hassle-free coverage.

9.7 Recommended Adaptive Travel Outfits

Here are ready-to-wear outfit ideas based on different travel scenarios:

✈ Airport & Long Travel Days

- Pull-on stretchable trousers – No buttons, no zippers, just comfort.

- Loose-fitted, moisture-wicking t-shirt – Reduces sweat buildup.

- Zip-front hoodie with deep pockets – Easy layering without overhead dressing.

- Slip-on sneakers or adaptive sandals – Avoids hassle at security checks.

👟 Adventure & Outdoor Travel

- Elastic-waist cargo pants with side zippers – Adjustable fit with accessible pockets.

- Quick-dry, breathable top – Minimizes discomfort in humidity.

- Poncho-style rain jacket – Hassle-free protection in unpredictable weather.

- Non-slip hiking sandals with Velcro straps – Ensures stability on uneven terrain.

Formal Dinners or Special Events

- Pre-stitched saree or stretchable fusion kurta – Maintains elegance with easy dressing.

- Adaptive formal blouse with front zippers – Eliminates small hook fastenings.

- Elasticated trousers or lehenga with an adjustable waistband – Accommodates long wear.

- Slip-on dress shoes or customized flats with extra padding – Avoids foot fatigue.

Beach & Resort Travel

- Swimwear with magnetic fastenings – Allows easy wear and removal.

- Kaftan or lightweight tunic with a front tie – Stylish and breezy.

- Slip-on water-resistant sandals – Hassle-free, even on sandy beaches.

- UV-protective hat with Velcro strap – Prevents sunburn without discomfort.

9.8 Adaptive Travel Outfits for Elderly Travelers

Elderly individuals often require clothing that prioritizes comfort, accessibility, and warmth while traveling. Adaptive features like easy closures, flexible waistbands, and breathable fabrics help reduce discomfort and make dressing easier.

Essentials for Elderly Travelers

- Elastic-Waist Bottoms – Avoids fumbling with zippers or buttons.

- Front-Zip or Magnetic Closure Tops – Eliminates the need for overhead dressing.

- Slip-On Shoes with Cushioned Insoles – Supports mobility without requiring bending.

- Temperature-Regulating Layers – Lightweight cardigans or shawls with Velcro fastenings for quick adjustments.

- Compression Socks for Circulation – Reduces swelling during long travel hours.

Recommended Travel Outfits for Seniors

✈ Airport or Long Travel Days

- Loose-Fit Joggers or Stretchable Cotton Pants (Elastic waistband, no fastenings).

- Soft, Wrinkle-Free Tunic or Front-Zip Cardigan (Easy layering for comfort).

- Slip-On Loafers with Arch Support (No laces or back straps).

Pre-Tied Scarf or Poncho (Lightweight yet warm).

🗇 Beach & Resort Wear

- Elastic-Waist Linen Pants or Adaptive Sarong (Breezy and adjustable).

- Front-Zip or Magnetic-Closure Cotton Blouse (No fiddly buttons).

- Lightweight Sun Hat with Adjustable Velcro Strap (Prevents slipping).

- Slip-On Sandals with Adjustable Straps (Ensures a secure fit without bending).

🗇 Formal Dinners & Gatherings

- Pre-Stitched Saree with Elastic Petticoat (No pleating needed).

- Adaptive Kurta with Side Openings or Magnetic Closures (Traditional yet easy to wear).

- Soft Leather or Stretchable Formal Shoes (Avoids discomfort for prolonged wear).

- Lightweight Dupatta with Shoulder Fasteners (Pre-attached to prevent slipping).

✉ Outdoor Sightseeing & Walking Tours

- Adaptive Trousers with Side Zippers (Allows easy adjustments for comfort).

- Long-Sleeve Breathable Cotton Shirt with Velcro Closures (Protects from sun & wind).

- Non-Slip Walking Shoes with Extra Cushioning (Reduces foot fatigue).

- Lightweight, Foldable Jacket with Easy Front Fastenings (Ensures warmth on-the-go).

9.9 Cultural Attire Adaptations for Travel

Many travelers prefer to wear traditional clothing while visiting religious or culturally significant places. However, traditional outfits can sometimes be restrictive, heavy, or difficult to manage. Here's how to adapt cultural attire for ease and accessibility while traveling:

Adaptive Indian Traditional Wear for Travel

☀ For Hot Climates:

- Pre-stitched cotton sarees with elastic waistbands & pre-pleated drapes.

- Lightweight, front-buttoned kurtas instead of heavy embroidered ones.

- Salwars & churidars with stretch panels for better mobility.

❄ For Cold Climates:

Wool-blend shawls with pre-sewn shoulder fasteners to prevent slipping.

Thermal leggings under sarees or salwars for warmth.

Poncho-style woolen shawls instead of heavy dupattas.

Adapting Modest Attire for Religious Travel

If traveling to temples, mosques, or churches, modest attire is often required. Here's how to make it more comfortable and accessible:

Velcro or magnetic-closure hijabs & scarves instead of traditional pins.

Full-length skirts with elastic waists instead of drawstrings for easier wear.

Kaftans with hidden side zippers for quick dressing.

Slip-on prayer caps & easy-tie turbans with pre-fixed pleats.

9.10 Packing Checklists for Different Climates

Packing for travel can be stressful, especially when managing accessibility needs. Here are adaptive travel packing lists tailored for various climates to ensure comfort, convenience, and independence.

✈ General Adaptive Travel Packing List

- **Wrinkle-Free Adaptive Clothing** – Magnetic closure shirts, pull-on pants, pre-stitched sarees, etc.

- **Slip-On Shoes & Extra Insoles** – Adaptive sandals or cushioned sneakers for long wear.

- **Compression Socks** – Reduces swelling on long flights or drives.

- **Lightweight Adaptive Outerwear** – Ponchos, shawls with fasteners, zippered cardigans.

- **Multi-Purpose Accessories** – Velcro-strap hats, easy-fasten scarves, pre-tied turbans.

- **Adaptive Luggage** – Suitcases with easy-grip handles, lightweight fabric, and multiple compartments.

- **Medical Essentials** – Travel-friendly pill organizers, cooling patches, and easy-access toiletry bags.

- **Backup Fastenings** – Extra Velcro strips, safety pins, fabric tape for quick repairs.

✳ Warm & Tropical Destinations (Beach, Summer Travel)

- Moisture-Wicking, Lightweight Fabrics – Bamboo, linen, or organic cotton.

- Loose-Fit Pants & Tunics – Elastic waistbands, side-zipped kurtas.

- Adaptive Swimwear – Magnetic or Velcro-fastened swimsuits, kaftans.

- Slip-On Water Shoes – Non-slip grip for wet surfaces.

- Pre-Fixed Sun Hats & UV Protection Clothing – Lightweight with Velcro fastenings.

- Cooling Accessories – Portable fans, sweat-wicking towels, cooling scarves.

🗇 Avoid: Heavy embroidery, dark colors, synthetic fabrics that trap heat.

✳ Cold Weather & Winter Travel

- Thermal Base Layers – Heat-retaining yet breathable.

- Fleece-Lined Pants & Adaptive Jackets –
  Zippered sides for easy dressing.

- Soft Wool or Fleece Accessories – Elasticated
  gloves, pre-tied scarves, Velcro shawls.

- Slip-On Boots with Extra Grip – Avoids
  tripping on icy surfaces.

- Heated Clothing – Battery-operated heating
  pads for jackets or gloves.

▢ Avoid: Heavy wool fabrics that irritate sensitive
skin, tight-fitting garments.

🌴 Rainy & Monsoon Travel

- Quick-Dry, Waterproof Clothing – Polyester-
  cotton blends, ponchos with side fastenings.

- Waterproof Slip-On Shoes – Lightweight, with
  non-slip soles.

- Pre-Stitched Wraps & Lightweight Shawls –
  Keeps you warm without bulk.

- Travel Umbrella with Easy Grip – Compact and
  accessible.

▢ Avoid: Long, flowy garments that may get caught
in puddles or mud.

9.11 Care Tips for Maintaining Adaptive Travel Clothing

Adaptive clothing should be durable, easy to wash, and maintainable on-the-go. Here are essential care tips:

Washing & Drying

- Use Gentle Detergents – Avoid harsh chemicals that can damage magnetic closures and soft fabrics.

- Hand-Wash Magnetic & Velcro Clothing – Prevents fabric weakening.

- Air-Dry Stretch Fabrics – Avoids shrinkage in high heat.

- Pack Travel Laundry Sheets – Lightweight, space-saving detergent strips for hand-washing clothes on-the-go.

Maintaining Fastenings & Modifications

- Check Velcro Strips Regularly – Clean lint buildup for better grip.

- Use Fabric Tape for Quick Fixes – Repair small tears without sewing.

- Keep Extra Magnetic Closures in a Travel Kit – In case replacements are needed.

Packing & Storing Adaptive Wear

- Roll, Don't Fold – Saves space and reduces wrinkles.

- Use Compression Packing Cubes – Keeps adaptive clothing organized.

- Store Shoes Separately in Zip Bags – Prevents dirt transfer.

9.12 Adaptive Travel Tips for Airports, Trains, and Road Trips

Traveling with adaptive clothing and accessibility needs requires planning. Whether flying, taking a train, or driving, these tips will help ensure a smooth journey.

✈ Airport & Flight Travel Tips

Before the Flight

- Request Special Assistance – Most airlines offer wheelchair assistance, priority boarding, and seating with extra legroom if booked in advance.

- Wear Easy-Fasten Clothing – Opt for elastic-waist pants, zippered sweaters, and slip-on shoes for quick security checks.

- Carry a Small Travel Kit – Pack compression socks, a neck pillow, and medications in a front-access bag.

- Use TSA-Approved Liquids Bags – Pre-pack adaptive toiletry items in a clear zip-lock bag for easy screening.

At Security Checkpoints

- Use Adaptive-Friendly Lanes – Some airports offer special lanes for wheelchair users and individuals with medical devices.

- Slip-On Shoes & Adaptive Belts – Avoid delays by wearing Velcro-fastened sneakers and belts without metal buckles.

- Notify Security About Medical Devices – If wearing compression braces or magnetic fastenings, inform security before screening.

During the Flight

- Stretch & Move Every 2 Hours – If mobility is limited, wiggle toes, rotate ankles, and shift positions to prevent stiffness.

- Use a Travel Blanket with Snap Fasteners – Ensures warmth without struggling with bulky fabric.

- Carry a Portable Urinal or Adaptive Toilet Aids – Some travelers find foldable toilet seats or handheld urinals helpful for long flights.

🗇 Train Travel Tips

Booking & Boarding

- Choose a Seat Near the Entrance – Trains often have priority seating for individuals with mobility issues.

- Carry a Lightweight, Adaptive Bag – Use a backpack with front-access zippers for easy storage and retrieval.

- Pack Non-Slip Slippers or Easy-Remove Shoes – Keeps feet comfortable during long journeys.

During the Journey

- Wear Adaptive Layers – Train temperatures can fluctuate, so bring a Velcro-fastened wrap or zip-up sweater.

- Use Noise-Canceling Headphones – Helps individuals with sensory sensitivities manage train noise.

- Book an Accessible Restroom-Friendly Seat – Some train routes offer wide-entry restrooms and priority access to washrooms.

🗐 Road Trip & Car Travel Tips

Pre-Trip Preparations

- Wear Compression Socks for Long Drives – Helps prevent swelling in feet and legs.

- Use a Memory Foam Travel Cushion – Reduces pressure on the lower back and joints.

- Pack an Adaptive Snack Kit – Carry pre-cut fruits, protein bars, and insulated bottles with easy-open lids.

On the Road

- Take Breaks Every 1.5 to 2 Hours – Stop for stretching, hydration, and restroom use.

- Wear Slip-Resistant Shoes – If getting in and out frequently, opt for easy-grip, Velcro-fastened shoes.

- Keep a Foldable Cane or Walker in the Car – If needed, store a compact, lightweight mobility aid for easy access.

For Adaptive Car Seating

- Use a Swivel Seat Cushion – Helps with easy entry and exit.

- Wear Loose, Elastic Clothing – Prevents stiffness during long rides.

- Carry an Emergency Medical Kit – Pack pain relief patches, heat packs, and quick-access medications.

9.13 Adaptive Hotel Stay Tips

A comfortable hotel stay depends on accessibility features, adaptive-friendly room arrangements, and thoughtful packing. Here's how to ensure a smooth experience.

Booking an Accessible Hotel Room

- Request a Ground-Floor or Elevator-Accessible Room – Reduces the need for stairs.

- Ensure the Bathroom is Wheelchair-Friendly – Ask for roll-in showers, grab bars, and raised toilet seats.

- Check for Bed Height & Accessibility – Some beds may be too high or too low for easy transfer.

- Confirm Adjustable AC & Lighting Controls – Remote-controlled features make adjustments easier.

Packing Essentials for a Comfortable Stay

- Portable Grab Bars or Suction Handles – Provides extra support in hotel bathrooms.

- Velcro-Closure Travel Pajamas – Makes nighttime dressing easier.

- Foldable Toilet Seat Riser – Useful if hotel toilets are too low.

- Portable Motion-Sensor Night Light – Prevents accidents in unfamiliar rooms.

Managing Hotel Stay Comfortably

- Arrange Furniture for Easy Mobility – Move chairs or tables for better wheelchair or walker access.

- Keep Essentials Near the Bed – Place medications, water, and assistive devices within arm's reach.

- Use Non-Slip Mats in the Bathroom – Reduces the risk of slipping on tiled floors.

- Inform Staff About Dietary Restrictions – If gluten-free or allergen-free meals are needed.

9.14 Accessible Sightseeing & Tourist Activities

Traveling to new destinations should be enjoyable, but some locations may not be fully accessible. Here's how to plan ahead for an inclusive and comfortable sightseeing experience.

Planning an Accessible Day Trip

- Research Wheelchair-Accessible Attractions – Many museums, heritage sites, and theme parks offer ramps, elevators, and reserved seating.

- Check Walking & Seating Availability – If long distances are involved, look for benches, shaded rest areas, or shuttle services.

- Book Skip-the-Line Passes – Many attractions allow priority access for individuals with mobility challenges.

- Pack an Adaptive Travel Kit – Include a cooling towel, lightweight rain poncho, and Velcro-fastened shoes for comfort.

Recommended Adaptive-Friendly Tourist Activities

❏ Cultural & Historical Sites

Opt for audio tours instead of guided walking tours.

Use pre-recorded virtual tours if mobility is limited.

Request assisted entry or priority seating for large events.

❏ Nature & Outdoor Travel

Choose wheelchair-friendly nature trails and boardwalks.

Wear compression sleeves or knee braces for long walks.

Bring portable seating stools for breaks on hiking routes.

❏ Shopping & City Exploration

Look for barrier-free malls with wheelchair ramps and elevators.

Use adaptive shopping trolleys with built-in seats for long shopping trips.

Wear lightweight adaptive shoes with arch support for all-day walking.

9.15 Adaptive Travel Tips for Cruises & International Travel

Cruises and international trips require extra planning, especially when managing mobility needs, accessibility, and cultural considerations. This section provides practical tips for an enjoyable, hassle-free journey.

🗇 Cruise Travel Tips for Accessibility & Comfort

Cruises are a great way to explore multiple destinations without frequent packing and unpacking. Most modern cruise ships offer accessibility features, but here's how to ensure a smooth experience:

Before Booking a Cruise

- Choose an Accessible Cabin – Request wider doors, roll-in showers, grab bars, and lower beds if needed.

- Ask About Onboard Accessibility – Check if elevators, ramps, and accessible dining areas are available.

- Look for Shore Excursions with Accessibility Options – Some cruise lines offer wheelchair-friendly sightseeing tours.

- Pack Adaptive Swimwear – Consider Velcro-fastened or zip-up swimsuits for pool accessibility.

Packing Essentials for a Cruise

- Non-Slip Sandals or Adaptive Water Shoes – Ideal for wet decks.

- Magnetic or Velcro-Closure Formal Wear – For dress-up nights.

- Compression Socks for Long Sailing Hours – Helps with circulation.

- Foldable Walking Stick or Cane Seat – Provides support during excursions.

- Motion Sickness Essentials – Anti-nausea bands, ginger candies, and travel sickness patches.

Managing Onboard Activities

- Use Room Service & Priority Dining – Reduces the need for walking long distances.

- Request Wheelchair Assistance for Shows & Events – Many theaters have priority seating.

- Use Adaptive Pool & Spa Features – Some ships have pool lifts and accessible spa areas.

- Book Early for Shore Excursions – Limited accessible tours fill up quickly.

✈ International Travel with Accessibility Needs

Traveling to another country requires extra planning for accessibility laws, transportation, and cultural adjustments.

Before the Trip

- Check the Destination's Accessibility Laws – Some countries have better accessibility than others. Research public transport, sidewalks, and building accessibility.

- Inform Airlines About Mobility Needs –
  Request wheelchair assistance, priority boarding,
  or special meals in advance.

- Carry Medical Documentation – Have a
  doctor's note for medications, medical devices,
  or dietary needs.

- Learn Key Local Phrases for Assistance – If
  traveling to a non-English-speaking country,
  carry a translation card with key phrases like:

"Where is the accessible entrance?"

"Can you assist me in getting to my seat?"

Packing for International Travel

- Adaptive Currency Holders – Velcro-sealed
  wallets for easy access to cash & cards.

- Pre-Mapped Accessible Routes – Use Google
  Maps' accessibility feature for step-free paths.

- Foldable Mobility Aids – Travel-friendly canes
  or walkers that fit in carry-ons.

- Portable Medication Cooler Bags – Essential
  for storing insulin, biologics, or temperature-
  sensitive medicines.

Navigating International Airports & Transit

- Request Assistance at Immigration & Customs –
  Many airports offer dedicated lines for travelers
  with disabilities.

- Choose Trains & Buses with Low-Floor Access
  – In some cities, accessible taxis or ride-sharing
  services are a better option.

- Check Hotel Accessibility Ahead of Time – Call ahead to confirm elevator access, bathroom modifications, and bed height.

🗇 Adapting to Different Cultures & Traditions

Different countries have unique customs regarding accessibility. Here are some cultural travel tips:

🗇 Middle East & South Asia

Traditional Attire Adaptations – Magnetic hijabs, pre-stitched sarees, and Velcro-closure kurtas make dressing easier.

Seating Arrangements – Some places use floor seating; pack a portable seat cushion if needed.

🗇 Europe

Cobbled Streets & Historic Sites – Many old cities have uneven pavements; use shock-absorbing shoe insoles for comfort.

Accessible Metro Systems – Research train stations with elevators and priority seating.

🗇 Japan & East Asia

Tatami Floor Adaptations – Some hotels use floor seating & sleeping; request low-rise beds if needed.

Public Transport Assistance – Many Japanese stations have "barrier-free" routes but require advance notice for assistance.

9.16 Accessible Dining Tips for Adaptive Travelers

Eating out while traveling can be a wonderful experience, but it can also present challenges for individuals with mobility limitations, dietary restrictions, or sensory sensitivities. Here's how to make dining more accessible and enjoyable.

🗐   Tips for Accessible Restaurant Dining

Before You Go

- Call Ahead to Check Accessibility – Ask about step-free entry, wheelchair-friendly seating, and accessible restrooms.

- Request a Table with Extra Space – For wheelchairs, walkers, or personal comfort, avoid tight booth seating.

- Confirm Special Dietary Accommodations – If gluten-intolerant, diabetic, or on a low-sodium diet, ask about meal adjustments.

At the Restaurant

- Choose Menus with Large Fonts or Digital Options – Easier to read for visual impairments.

- Use Adaptive Cutlery or Request Soft-Grip Utensils – Some restaurants provide ergonomic forks, knives, and straws.

- Order Foods That Are Easy to Eat – If dexterity is an issue, opt for dishes without excessive cutting or peeling.

Packing an Adaptive Dining Kit

- Non-Slip Placemats – Keeps plates stable on tables.

- Silicone-Tipped Straws – Useful for those with jaw or hand mobility limitations.

- Folding Travel Utensils with Large Grips – Helps with independent eating.

- Small Seasoning Packets – Carry salt, sugar, or gluten-free soy sauce for flavor adjustments.

🗇 Adaptive Eating for Street Food & Buffets

🗇 Street Food

- Choose Vendors with Seating Options – If mobility is limited, find stalls with stools or standing counters.

- Ask for Smaller Portions – If eating while walking, bite-sized snacks or skewered foods are easier to handle.

- Use Disposable Utensils with a Grip Wrap – Adds comfort when handling plastic cutlery.

🗇 Buffet Dining

- Ask for Assistance at Serving Stations – Many buffets allow staff to help fill plates.

- Use Lightweight, Stackable Plates – Reduces the strain of carrying heavy dishes.

- Look for Allergen Labels – Many buffets mark common allergens like nuts, dairy, and gluten.

9.17 Emergency Preparedness for Adaptive Travelers

Emergencies can happen anywhere, so it's important to have a safety plan in place while traveling.

◻ Emergency Packing Essentials

- Medical Alert ID or Card – Lists conditions, medications, allergies, and emergency contacts.

- Portable First Aid Kit – Includes bandages, antiseptic wipes, and basic medications.

- Backup Mobility Aids – If using a cane, walker, or wheelchair, pack a foldable spare.

- Universal Power Adapter & Portable Charger – Ensures medical devices or emergency contacts stay powered.

- Pre-Written Emergency Translations – Helps in non-English-speaking countries (e.g., "I need medical assistance").

- Small Emergency Food Supply – Gluten-free or allergen-friendly snacks if dietary needs are strict.

◻ Handling Medical Emergencies While Traveling

◻ If You Need Medical Help

- Know the Nearest Hospitals & Pharmacies – Research accessible medical centers before your trip.

- Download an Emergency Health App – Some apps translate medical conditions into local languages.

- Carry a Doctor's Note for Medications – Especially for controlled substances like painkillers or insulin.

🗇 If You're in a Travel Accident

- Have Travel Insurance with Medical Coverage – Ensure it covers mobility aids, wheelchair damage, or hospital stays.

- Inform Travel Companions About Emergency Plans – Share a list of allergies, medications, and emergency contacts.

- Keep an Emergency Whistle or Flashlight – Useful for power outages, nighttime travel, or getting attention.

Chapter 10

DIY Adaptive Fashion Hacks for Everyday Wear

Adaptive clothing doesn't always have to be custom-made. Many everyday garments can be modified at home with simple DIY techniques to improve accessibility, comfort, and style. This chapter provides easy, budget-friendly hacks to transform regular clothes into adaptive wear.

10.1 No – Sew Adaptive Clothing Modifications

Not everyone has access to a sewing machine, so here are no-sew methods to make clothing more functional and accessible.

Replace Buttons with Velcro or Magnets

- Use Fabric Glue to Attach Velcro Strips – Instead of sewing, attach self-adhesive or iron-on Velcro behind button plackets.

- Glue or Clip Magnets Inside the Fabric – Creates invisible, easy-to-close fastenings for shirts and jackets.

- Use Decorative Button Covers – Keeps the original look while hiding adaptive closures underneath.

Turn Jeans into Elastic-Waist Pants

- Remove the Front Button & Zipper – Replace with stretchable waistband fabric or elastic drawstrings.

- Use a Hair Tie for Extra Flexibility – Loop a rubber band or hair tie around the buttonhole to create an adjustable waistband.

- Cut Side Slits & Add Fabric Tape – Allows extra hip movement for wheelchair users.

Transform Traditional Wear into Adaptive Outfits

- Pre-Stitch Saree Pleats & Add a Hidden Zip – Makes sarees ready-to-wear like a skirt.

- Convert Kurtas & Anarkalis into Front-Open Designs – Use stick-on snap buttons or zippers.

- Attach Magnetic Clips to Dupattas – Prevents them from slipping off shoulders.

10.2 DIY Modifications for Footwear

Adaptive shoes can be expensive, but small modifications can make regular footwear easier to wear.

Convert Lace-Up Shoes to Slip-Ons

- Replace Shoelaces with Elastic Laces – Allows feet to slide in without tying knots.

- Use a Zipper Side Closure – Sew or glue a zipper along the shoe's side for easy access.

- Attach Velcro Fasteners Instead of Laces – Ensures a secure grip without the effort of tying.

Modify Slippers & Sandals for Comfort

- Use Soft, Padded Insoles – Adds extra cushioning for foot pain or sensitivity.

- Attach Heel Straps with Velcro – Provides a better grip for loose-fitting sandals.

- Add Non-Slip Rubber Grips – Prevents falls for elderly or mobility-challenged individuals.

10.3 Simple Hacks for Dressing Independence

Dressing should be as easy and stress-free as possible. Here are DIY techniques for improving clothing accessibility.

One-Hand Dressing Techniques

- Attach a Loop to Zippers – Use a keyring, ribbon, or fabric loop to make pulling zippers easier.

- Use a Button Hook for Shirts – Helps fasten buttons with one hand.

- Wear Pre-Stitched Ties & Scarves – Reduces the need for manual tying.

Modifications for Limited Mobility

- Sew Side Openings in Trousers – Makes them easier to step into.

- Attach Extended Pull Tabs to Jackets – Helps those with limited hand strength zip up coats.

- Convert Regular Tops into Open-Back Designs – Use Velcro or snap closures for easy wear.

10.4 DIY Adaptive Clothing Hacks for Kids

Children with mobility challenges, sensory sensitivities, or dexterity difficulties often need adaptive clothing that is easy to wear, soft on the skin, and adjustable for growth. These DIY hacks help parents modify regular clothes into comfortable, accessible, and stylish adaptive wear for kids.

- Modifying Everyday Clothing for Easy Dressing

- Convert T-Shirts into Front-Opening Styles

  - Use Fabric Tape or Velcro Instead of Pull-Over Designs – Cut along the back or front and attach Velcro or snap buttons to create an easy-on, easy-off shirt.

  - Magnetic Closures for Quick Dressing – Replace tight neck openings with magnetic fastenings.

- Elastic-Waist Bottoms for Independent Dressing

  - Replace Zippers & Buttons with Wide Elastic Bands – Allows kids to pull pants on/off easily.

  - Use Side Snaps for Changing Ease – Add Velcro strips or snaps along the side seams of trousers or leggings.

  - Adjustable Drawstrings with Cord Locks – Prevents pants from being too loose or tight.

- Sensory-Friendly School Uniform Hacks

  - Tag-Free & Flat-Seam Clothing – Use a seam ripper to remove scratchy tags or stitch flat seams to prevent irritation.

- Soft, Breathable Fabrics – Replace itchy polyester uniforms with cotton linings inside shirts and pants.

- Pre-Tied School Ties & Shoes – Reduces the need for fine motor coordination during dressing.

- Adaptive Footwear Hacks for Kids

- No-Tie Shoe Solutions

  - Replace Laces with Elastic or Locking Shoelaces – Allows kids to slip shoes on without tying.

  - Add Velcro Straps to Sneakers – Modify regular sneakers with stick-on or sewn Velcro for quick fastening.

  - Use Zippers on the Side of Boots – Makes boots easier to slip on and off.

- Preventing Sensory Discomfort in Shoes

  - Use Padded Insoles for Soft Support – Reduces pressure on sensitive feet.

  - Sew Soft Lining into Stiff Shoe Backs – Prevents rubbing and blisters.

  - Use Non-Slip Stickers for Stability – Adds grip to help kids walk safely on slippery floors.

- Adaptive School Accessories & Outerwear

- Easy-Access School Bags

  - Backpacks with Front Openings – Use zippers that fully open in the front for quick access.

- Adjustable Straps with Quick-Release Buckles
  – Allows kids to wear and remove backpacks
  easily.

- Attach Key Clips Inside Bags – Helps kids keep
  track of essentials like ID cards and small items.

🗐 Adaptive Jackets & Sweaters

- Convert Regular Jackets to Velcro-Closure
  Coats – Replace buttons with Velcro or magnets
  for easy fastening.

- Attach Extended Zip Pulls – Helps kids zip up
  coats independently.

- Use Poncho-Style Raincoats – Eliminates the
  need for complicated arm movements when
  wearing a raincoat.

🗐 Adaptive Hacks for Infants & Toddlers

🗐 Quick-Change Baby Onesies & Pajamas

- Use Magnetic or Velcro Closures Instead of
  Snaps – Reduces dressing time for parents of
  infants with special needs.

- Convert Onesies into Adaptive Bodysuits – Add
  side openings for medical ports or feeding tubes.

🗐 Easy-Access Bibs & Feeding Clothing

- Slip-On or Velcro-Fastened Bibs – Avoids tight
  neck closures.

- Waterproof, Stain-Resistant Fabrics – Helps kids
  stay dry and comfortable during feeding.

10.5 Seasonal Adaptive Clothing Hacks for Kids

Children's clothing needs change with the seasons, but kids with mobility challenges, sensory sensitivities, or fine motor difficulties may struggle with traditional seasonal wear. These DIY seasonal hacks ensure that children stay comfortable, warm, or cool while maintaining ease of dressing and movement.

☀ Summer Adaptive Clothing Hacks

❒ Lightweight, Breathable Fabrics

- Replace Heavy School Uniforms with Cotton Linings – If uniforms are required, stitch soft, moisture-wicking cotton inside polyester shirts to prevent overheating.

- Cut-Off Sleeves for Hot Days – Convert full-sleeve shirts into short-sleeve, loose-fitting tops for better airflow.

❒ Easy-On Summer Shoes

- Convert Sandals to Velcro-Fastened Slip-Ons – Replace buckle closures with adjustable Velcro straps.

- Sew Soft Fabric into Flip-Flop Straps – Prevents irritation for kids sensitive to rubbing.

❒ Sun Protection Modifications

- Pre-Tied, Easy-Wrap Sun Hats – Use Velcro under the chin instead of difficult tie straps.

- Sew Cooling Towels Inside Caps – Keeps kids cool during outdoor activities.

- Lightweight Poncho-Style Cover-Ups – Quick, pull-over protection for swimming or outdoor play.

❄ Winter Adaptive Clothing Hacks

🗇 Sensory-Friendly Layering

- Tag-Free, Soft-Fabric Inner Layers – Remove itchy wool tags and replace scratchy seams with flat stitches.

- Attach Thermal Leggings to Pants – Prevents layers from shifting when worn by active children.

- Convert Hoodies into Magnetic-Zip Jackets – Makes zipping up coats easier for kids with fine motor difficulties.

🗇 Adaptive Gloves & Mittens

- Magnetic or Velcro-Fastened Mittens – Replaces tight-fitting wristbands for quick removal.

- Use Elastic Cuffs Instead of Drawstrings – Prevents kids from struggling with pulling mittens over sleeves.

🗇 Heated Accessories for Warmth

- Sew Heating Pads into Jackets – Small, battery-operated warming patches help keep kids cozy.

- Fleece-Lined Socks with Adjustable Fasteners – Keeps feet warm without causing discomfort.

- Poncho-Style Wool Coats for Wheelchair Users
    – Easier than traditional zip-up jackets.

- Rainy & Monsoon Adaptive Clothing Hacks

- Waterproof Clothing Modifications

  - Convert Raincoats into Poncho-Style Covers –
    Makes putting on and taking off easier.

  - Use Magnetic or Velcro Closures Instead of
    Zippers – Helps kids who struggle with zipping
    jackets.

  - Elastic Ankles for Rain Pants – Prevents mud
    and water from splashing inside pant legs.

- Adaptive Rain Shoes

  - Non-Slip, Easy-Fasten Rain Boots – Add elastic
    pull-loops for easy slip-on wear.

  - Waterproof Shoe Covers for Kids in
    Wheelchairs – Keeps feet dry without needing
    to remove shoes.

- Sensory-Friendly Rain Gear

  - Soft-Lined Rain Hats – Reduces sensory
    discomfort from plastic rain gear.

  - Breathable, Quick-Dry Fabrics – Avoids sticky
    or clingy materials that may irritate sensitive
    skin.

- Spring & Autumn Adaptive Clothing Hacks

- Transition-Weather Layers

  - Sew Light Fleece Linings into Shirts – Adds
    warmth without bulky layering.

- Use Zip-Off Sleeves for Changing Weather –
    Creates convertible jackets and sweatshirts.

- Footwear for Changing Temperatures

  - Adjustable Sneakers for Swelling Feet – Use
      elastic bands instead of traditional laces.

  - Attach Non-Slip Patches to Shoe Soles –
      Prevents slips on wet autumn leaves.

- Easy-Remove Jackets & Sweaters

  - Replace Tight Necklines with Stretch Panels –
      Makes pulling over heads easier.

  - Use Reversible, Double-Layer Jackets – Allows
      quick changes based on the weather.

10.6 Festival & Special Occasion Adaptive Clothing Hacks for Kids

Festivals and special occasions often require traditional or formal attire, which can be difficult for children with mobility limitations, sensory sensitivities, or fine motor challenges. These DIY adaptive clothing hacks ensure that kids can dress comfortably and independently while celebrating special events.

- Adaptive Traditional Wear for Indian Festivals

- Sarees & Lehengas for Girls

  - Pre-Stitched Lehengas with Elastic Waistbands
      – Replaces heavy, zippered or drawstring skirts
      with soft, stretchable waistbands.

- Magnetic or Velcro-Fastened Blouses – Makes it easier for kids to wear cholis without struggling with hooks.

- Pre-Draped Sarees – Convert sarees into ready-to-wear skirts with attached pleats and pallu.

- Lightweight Dupattas with Shoulder Fasteners – Use snap buttons or magnets to prevent dupattas from slipping.

❒ Kurtas & Sherwanis for Boys

- Replace Front Buttons with Hidden Velcro or Magnets – Keeps the traditional look while making dressing easier.

- Use Elastic-Waist Pajamas & Salwars – Eliminates the need for drawstring ties.

- Zippered or Side-Opening Sherwanis – Makes getting in and out of heavy embroidered outfits easier.

- Attach Secure Clips for Turbans or Pagris – Pre-tied Velcro turbans prevent them from slipping.

❒ Adaptive Hacks for Christmas, Easter, & Western Festivities

❒ Comfortable & Accessible Party Wear

- Stretchable Formal Dresses with Hidden Side Zippers – Allows kids to slip into dresses without overhead movement.

- Clip-On Bowties & Pre-Tied Neckties – Removes the need for tying knots.

- Elastic-Waist Dress Pants for Boys – Provides a formal look with adaptive comfort.
- Magnetic or Velcro Shirt Closures – Helps kids avoid struggling with tiny buttons.

🗐 Sensory-Friendly Festive Clothing

- Remove Itchy Seams & Tags from Party Dresses – Stitch a soft cotton lining inside fancy dresses.
- Use Lightweight, Non-Irritating Fabrics – Opt for soft cotton, silk blends, or modal instead of scratchy sequins.
- Soft-Fabric Tights & Socks – Use seamless, stretchable leggings instead of tight-fitting stockings.

🗐 Adaptive Hacks for Fancy Dress, Halloween, & Costume Events

🗐 Easy-Wear Costumes for Kids with Mobility Challenges

- Poncho-Style Costumes – Creates no-fuss superhero capes, fairy wings, or character outfits.
- Zippered or Velcro-Back Costumes – Makes dressing and undressing simple.
- Wheelchair-Accessible Costume Hacks – Use fabric panels and lightweight props to integrate wheelchairs into costumes (e.g., a chariot or spaceship design).

🗐 Sensory-Friendly Halloween & Dress-Up Outfits

- Use Soft Face Paint Instead of Masks – Avoids tight, itchy elastic bands.

  - Cotton-Lined Costumes – Reduces irritation from synthetic or scratchy materials.

  - Magnetic or Snap-Button Capes & Wings – Allows kids to remove them easily if they feel uncomfortable.

- Adaptive Birthday Party & Wedding Outfits

- Party Dresses & Tuxedos

  - Stretchable, Tag-Free Birthday Dresses – Opt for soft cotton or jersey fabric instead of stiff satin.

  - Clip-On Bow Ties & Velcro Suspenders – Keeps a formal look without tricky fastenings.

  - Hidden Elastic Inserts for Formal Wear – Allows kids to move freely without tight clothing restrictions.

- Wheelchair-Friendly Formal Wear

  - Pre-Sewn Gowns with Open-Back Designs – Makes dressing easier for kids who use wheelchairs.

  - Adjustable Length Dresses – Use snap buttons inside the hem to shorten or extend dresses.

  - Flat-Seam & Tag-Free Formal Clothes – Reduces sensory irritation during long events.

10.7 Adaptive Festival Accessories & Footwear Hacks for Kids

Festive outfits aren't complete without accessories and footwear, but traditional shoes, jewelry, and headwear can sometimes be uncomfortable or difficult for children with mobility or sensory challenges. These adaptive hacks ensure that accessories are comfortable, secure, and easy to wear.

🗐 Adaptive Accessories for Festivals & Special Events

🗐 Easy-Fasten Jewelry & Hair Accessories

- Magnetic or Velcro Bracelets & Bangles – Eliminates clasp struggles for kids with limited dexterity.

- Pre-Tied Hairbands & Clips – Avoids tight elastics and painful pulling on sensitive scalps.

- Clip-On or Magnetic Earrings – Provides a non-piercing alternative for festive looks.

- Stretchable Beaded Necklaces – Uses elastic string instead of traditional clasps.

🗐 Festival-Ready Dupattas & Scarves

- Pre-Attached Dupattas for Girls – Sew one end of the dupatta to the dress or lehenga blouse to keep it secure.

- Snap Button Dupatta Holders – Prevents scarves from slipping off during movement.

- Lightweight, Cotton-Lined Dupattas – Reduces sensory discomfort from heavy, embroidered fabrics.

🗇 Adaptive Turbans & Headgear for Boys

- Pre-Tied Turbans with Velcro Straps – Keeps pagris and Sikh turbans secure without traditional tying.

- Lightweight, Foam-Filled Headgear – Reduces pressure on the forehead for longer wear.

- Soft-Fabric Crowns for Birthday Parties – Use stretchable headbands instead of stiff plastic crowns.

🗇 Adaptive Festive Footwear for Kids

🗇 Comfortable Traditional Footwear

- Elastic-Back Juttis & Mojaris – Instead of rigid back straps, use stretchable bands for easy slip-on.

- Velcro-Strap Sandals Instead of Buckles – Reduces difficulty with fastenings.

- Soft-Lined, Cushioned Shoes – Adds a layer of memory foam to prevent irritation from stiff soles.

🗇 Non-Slip & Stability-Enhancing Shoes

- Non-Slip Stickers for Dress Shoes – Helps prevent skidding on smooth floors.

- Flat, Padded Soles Instead of Hard Leather – Enhances comfort for prolonged wear.

- Velcro-Added Kolhapuri Chappals & Sandals
  – Converts traditional footwear into easy-
  fastening designs.

🗇 Sensory-Friendly Footwear Solutions

- Tag-Free, Soft-Fabric Shoe Linings – Prevents
  itchiness inside closed shoes.

- Stretchable, Sock-Like Party Shoes – Provides
  flexibility for kids who dislike tight footwear.

- Slip-On Dress Shoes with Adjustable Fit – Uses
  hidden elastic bands for customized comfort.

10.8 DIY Adaptive Festival Props & Costume Hacks for Kids

Festivals, school performances, and cultural events often require props, costume add-ons, and themed outfits. However, these can sometimes be heavy, uncomfortable, or difficult to manage for children with mobility or sensory challenges. These DIY adaptive hacks ensure that kids can fully participate while staying comfortable and confident.

🗇 Lightweight & Adaptive Festival Props

🗇 Easy-to-Hold Handheld Props

- Use Soft Foam Instead of Heavy Materials –
  Replace wooden or plastic props with foam,
  cardboard, or lightweight fabric-wrapped
  designs.

- Attach Wrist Straps for Grip Support – If a child
  struggles to hold props, add an adjustable wrist
  strap for security.

- Magnetic or Velcro Grips for Accessories – For wands, swords, or festive sticks, attach a Velcro loop for easy grip without effort.

🗗 Wheelchair-Integrated Props & Costumes

- Create Costume Extensions for Wheelchairs – Convert the chair into a chariot, royal throne, or superhero vehicle using lightweight cardboard panels.

- Use Clip-On Fabric Panels Instead of Heavy Add-Ons – For festive parades, attach lightweight fabric capes or banners to the wheelchair instead of bulky props.

- Add LED Light Strips for a Festive Touch – Battery-operated string lights can make festival props vibrant without adding weight.

🗗 Sensory-Friendly Costumes for School & Festive Events

🗗 Soft & Adaptive Fancy Dress Costumes

- Replace Zippers with Velcro or Magnetic Closures – Makes dressing and undressing quick and effortless.

- Use Cotton or Bamboo Linings for Itchy Costumes – Prevents discomfort from sequin, lace, or synthetic fabric outfits.

- Stretchable Waistbands for Long-Wear Comfort – Adds flexibility for kids in traditional or tight-fitted costumes.

- Use Pre-Tied Capes & Cloaks Instead of Neck Ties – Velcro-sealed capes prevent choking risks.

🗇 DIY Festival-Themed Adaptive Costumes

🗇 Krishna or Ramayana Costumes

Use Magnetic Jewelry Instead of Tied Beads – Allows quick dressing without clasps.

Lightweight Crowns with Adjustable Headbands – Avoids heavy metal-based designs.

Velcro-Fastened Dhotis & Dupattas – Makes traditional outfits easy to wear.

🗇 Superhero or Mythological Warrior Costumes

Elastic Wristbands Instead of Strap-On Gauntlets – Allows kids to move freely without restrictive straps.

Foam Shields & Weapons – Keeps props lightweight and safe for play.

Easy-Wear Chest Plates with Velcro – Instead of tight rope ties, use adjustable Velcro straps.

🗇 Princess, Fairy, & Angel Costumes

Attach Wings with Soft Shoulder Loops – Instead of straps that dig into the skin.

Use Clip-On Tiaras & Crowns – Eliminates hard plastic that may cause discomfort.

Adjustable Tulle Skirts with Soft Elastic Bands – Keeps fancy dresses comfortable for long events.

🗇 Safe & Accessible Festival Accessories for Kids

- ⬚ Light-Up Festival Accessories

  - Battery-Powered Glow Accessories Instead of Candles – Use glow sticks, LED wristbands, or fiber-optic wands for Diwali, Christmas, or Halloween.

  - Clip-On Light-Up Earrings & Bangles – Safe for sensory-sensitive kids who dislike regular jewelry.

- ⬚ Festival-Themed Caps & Headgear

  - Soft, Adjustable Hats for Themed Events – Use lightweight, elastic-fitted caps for traditional looks.

  - DIY Soft-Fabric Halos & Headbands – Perfect for nativity plays, Christmas angels, or fairy costumes.

Chapter 11

The Future of Adaptive Fashion in India

Adaptive fashion in India is still an evolving industry, but the demand for inclusive, stylish, and accessible clothing is rapidly growing. This chapter explores the current landscape, innovations, and future possibilities in adaptive fashion, highlighting how India can become a global leader in affordable, culturally relevant, and functional adaptive wear.

11.1 The Current State of Adaptive Fashion in India

Unlike Western countries, where adaptive fashion brands have gained mainstream attention, India's market for accessible clothing is still in its early stages. However, with a large ageing population, growing awareness of disability rights, and increased demand for comfortable wear, the industry is poised for transformation.

🗇 Challenges in India's Adaptive Fashion Industry

- Lack of Awareness & Availability – Few Indian brands specialize in adaptive traditional and contemporary clothing.

- High Cost of Imported Adaptive Clothing – Many global adaptive brands are expensive and inaccessible to the average Indian consumer.

- Limited Representation in Retail & E-Commerce – Most mainstream stores and online platforms do not cater to people with disabilities or mobility challenges.

- Lack of Tailoring Services for Adaptive Wear – Even though India has a strong tailoring culture, most tailors are not trained in adaptive clothing modifications.

❐ Emerging Opportunities in Adaptive Fashion

- Incorporating Traditional Indian Wear into Adaptive Designs – Making sarees, kurtas, lehengas, and sherwanis more accessible.

- Growing Demand for Elderly & Medical Clothing – With an aging population, there is a rising need for easy-dress clothing for seniors.

- The Rise of Inclusive Fashion Startups – New homegrown brands are exploring adaptive clothing solutions.

- Government & NGO Involvement – Organizations are promoting skill training for adaptive fashion tailors.

11.2 Innovations in Adaptive Fashion

❐ Technological Advancements

- Smart Fabrics for Temperature Regulation – Clothes that adapt to body temperature changes, beneficial for people with sensory sensitivities or chronic illnesses.

- AI-Based Custom Tailoring – Using 3D scanning and AI technology to design personalized adaptive clothing.

- Self-Fastening Garments with Motion Sensors – Smart wearables that can adjust fit automatically based on movement.

🗇 Affordable Adaptive Wear Innovations in India

- Pre-Stitched, Elasticated Traditional Wear – Ready-to-wear sarees, lehengas, and kurtas with built-in stretch and fastenings.

- Magnetic & Velcro-Closure Clothing at Budget Prices – Adapting fastenings to suit Indian markets.

- Bamboo & Herbal Dyed Fabrics for Skin Sensitivities – Organic fabrics that prevent skin irritation and allergies.

11.3 The Future of Inclusive Fashion in India

🗇 Making Adaptive Fashion More Accessible

- Expanding Adaptive Clothing in Retail Stores – Encouraging big brands like Fabindia, Biba, and Manyavar to introduce adaptive ethnic wear.

- Training Local Tailors in Adaptive Modifications – Providing workshops to make adaptive alterations widely available.

- Government Initiatives & Tax Benefits – Encouraging policies that support affordable adaptive clothing production.

❑ Changing Social Attitudes Towards Adaptive Fashion

- Greater Representation in Fashion Shows & Advertising – Featuring models with disabilities and elderly individuals in campaigns.

- Promoting Adaptive Fashion in Schools & Colleges – Creating awareness about inclusive design principles among fashion students.

- Celebrating Adaptive Clothing as a Style Statement – Moving away from "functional-only" designs to trendy, aesthetic adaptive fashion.

11.4 Case Studies: Indian Adaptive Fashion Brands & Initiatives

Several Indian designers and brands have started exploring adaptive clothing, blending functionality with cultural aesthetics. These case studies highlight pioneers in inclusive fashion, showcasing how India is adapting to the growing need for accessible clothing.

❑ Case Study 1: 'Bunaai' – Pre-Stitched Sarees for Easy Draping

❑ Overview:

Bunaai, a Jaipur-based brand, is known for its lightweight ethnic wear. While not exclusively adaptive, the brand introduced pre-stitched sarees that require minimal pleating, making them ideal for women with mobility challenges or arthritis.

❑ Adaptive Features:

- Pre-Pleated Saree Skirts – Worn like a wrap-around skirt, eliminating the need for intricate pleating.

- Elasticated Petticoats for Adjustable Fit – Comfortable for weight fluctuations and easy pull-on wear.

- Magnetic or Snap Closure Pallus – Secures the saree drape without pins.

❑ Impact:

Many elderly women and individuals with dexterity issues have adopted these pre-stitched sarees for everyday use.

The concept has encouraged mainstream ethnic brands to explore adaptive saree designs.

❑ Case Study 2: 'Aara By Avantika' – Adaptive Occasion Wear

❑ Overview:

Aara By Avantika is a boutique brand that customizes wedding and festive attire for individuals with limited mobility, prosthetics, or wheelchair use.

❑ Adaptive Features:

- Sherwanis & Lehengas with Hidden Side Zippers – Allows step-in dressing without lifting arms.

- Kurta Sets with Elastic or Magnetic Closures – Instead of traditional buttons.

- Lightweight Bridal Wear for Long Events –
  Reducing the weight of embroidered fabrics.

🗗 Impact:

Featured in Indian bridal fashion circles as an inclusive
wedding wear pioneer.

Created awareness that adaptive fashion can still be
glamorous and trendy.

🗗 Case Study 3: 'Ability People' – India's First
Adaptive Clothing Brand

🗗 Overview:

Ability People, based in Hyderabad, is India's first
dedicated adaptive clothing brand, focusing on paralysis,
post-surgery wear, and disability-friendly garments.

🗗 Adaptive Features:

- Open-Back & Side-Opening Shirts for Easy
  Dressing.

- Adaptive Inner-wear with Soft Closures for
  Comfort.

- Medical Access Clothing for People with IV
  Ports & Prosthetics.

🗗 Impact:

Highlighted in national disability forums as a game-
changer for accessibility in Indian fashion.

Inspired more regional startups to enter the adaptive
fashion space.

🗗 Case Study 4: 'Utsa by Westside' – Affordable,
  Easy-Wear Everyday Clothing

- Overview:

Utsa by Westside has introduced loose-fitted, elasticated tunics and kurtas that are not marketed as adaptive but are widely used by elderly women and individuals with mobility limitations.

- Adaptive Features:

  - Slip-On Kurtas with No Fastenings – Eliminates the need for zippers or buttons.

  - Stretchable Fabrics for Flexible Fit – Accommodates weight changes and post-surgery wear.

  - Soft, Tag-Free Designs for Sensory Comfort – Prevents skin irritation.

- Impact:

One of the first major Indian retail brands to create naturally adaptive-friendly designs at budget prices.

Helped normalize comfortable, non-restrictive ethnic wear in mainstream fashion.

- Case Study 5: 'Ramp My City' – Inclusive Fashion Events

- Overview:

Ramp My City is a Bangalore-based initiative that showcases models with disabilities on the runway, promoting adaptive fashion brands.

- Achievements:

  - Organized India's First Adaptive Fashion Show.

- Collaborated with Local Designers to Modify Traditional Wear.
- Raised Awareness About the Need for Inclusive Fashion in India.

❒ Impact:

Increased visibility of adaptive fashion in Indian media.

Encouraged big brands to rethink accessibility in their designs.

11.5 Lessons from Indian Adaptive Fashion Pioneers

These case studies highlight key takeaways for the future of adaptive fashion in India:

- Mainstream brands should integrate adaptive features in their designs, not as a separate category.
- More traditional clothing options (like sarees, lehengas, and sherwanis) should be made adaptive.
- Regional tailors and designers need training in adaptive modifications.
- Awareness campaigns can drive demand and increase accessibility for the masses.

11.6 Government Policies & Initiatives Supporting Adaptive Fashion in India

India has made significant progress in promoting inclusivity, accessibility, and disability rights, but the adaptive fashion industry still requires stronger policy support. This section explores government initiatives, legal frameworks, and potential policy improvements to make adaptive clothing more accessible and affordable.

- ❒ Existing Government Policies Related to Adaptive Fashion

- ❒ The Rights of Persons with Disabilities (RPWD) Act, 2016

The RPWD Act, 2016 mandates equal opportunities and accessibility for individuals with disabilities. While it primarily focuses on infrastructure, education, and employment, it also encourages industries like fashion, retail, and design to create inclusive products.

How It Supports Adaptive Fashion:

- Promotes Inclusion in Workspaces – Encourages brands to hire persons with disabilities in fashion and textile industries.

- Encourages Accessibility in Retail Spaces – Ensures shopping malls and stores are wheelchair-friendly.

- Allows Tax Benefits for Disability-Oriented Businesses – Adaptive fashion brands may qualify for financial incentives.

- ❒ Make in India & Skill India Initiatives

The Make in India and Skill India programs focus on enhancing local manufacturing and providing specialized skill training.

How It Supports Adaptive Fashion:

- Encourages Adaptive Clothing Production in India – Reduces dependency on expensive imported adaptive wear.

- Provides Tailoring Training for Adaptive Designs – Government-run skill centers could train tailors in modifying garments for accessibility.

🗗 GST & Tax Benefits for Disability-Related Products

Currently, mobility aids, prosthetics, and assistive devices are taxed at 5% under GST instead of the standard 18%. However, adaptive clothing is not yet classified under this category.

Potential Policy Improvements:

- Lower GST for Adaptive Clothing – If included under assistive devices, adaptive fashion could become more affordable.

- Subsidised Fabric Costs for Adaptive Fashion Designers – Making specialized, disability-friendly fabrics cheaper for Indian designers.

🗗 Government Programs That Can Be Expanded to Include Adaptive Fashion

🗗 Sugamya Bharat Abhiyan (Accessible India Campaign)

This initiative aims to make public spaces, transport, and digital platforms more accessible. However, fashion and clothing accessibility are not yet included.

🗗 Proposal for Adaptive Fashion Inclusion:

- Encourage Government Tenders for Adaptive School Uniforms & Workwear.

- Introduce Adaptive Clothing Guidelines in Public Sector Companies.

- Include Adaptive Fashion in Government-Led Startup Grants.

🗐 National Handloom Development Program (NHDP)

India has a rich tradition of handloom textiles, but adaptive clothing remains a niche area. The NHDP promotes regional artisans and fabric innovation.

🗐 Proposal for Adaptive Fashion Inclusion:

- Create a Handloom-Based Adaptive Clothing Line – Lightweight, breathable khadi, muslin, and silk fabrics can be adapted into sensory-friendly Indian wear.

- Provide Grants for Traditional Weavers to Learn Adaptive Modifications – Training artisans to create accessible ethnic wear.

🗐 The Future: Policy Recommendations for Adaptive Fashion Growth

To make adaptive clothing affordable, accessible, and widely available in India, policymakers should consider:

- Incentives for Local Designers Creating Adaptive Wear – Financial support for homegrown adaptive brands.

- Public-Private Partnerships for Large-Scale Production – Encouraging major brands like

Fabindia, Biba, Manyavar to create adaptive lines.

- Adaptive Fashion Training for Design Institutes – Introducing adaptive fashion courses in NIFT (National Institute of Fashion Technology).

- Subsidies for Adaptive School Uniforms & Workplace Clothing – Making inclusive fashion more affordable for students and professionals.

11.7 Consumer Awareness & Accessibility in Indian Retail

Despite growing conversations around adaptive fashion, many Indian consumers remain unaware of accessible clothing options. This section explores how brands, designers, and advocacy groups can increase awareness and ensure adaptive fashion reaches mainstream retail markets.

🗇 Challenges in Retail Accessibility for Adaptive Fashion

🗇 Limited In-Store Availability

- Most major fashion retailers do not stock adaptive wear, making it difficult for consumers to explore and try products before purchasing.

- Brands like Fabindia, Biba, and Westside offer comfortable, loose-fitted clothing, but lack dedicated adaptive sections.

🗇 High Reliance on Custom Tailoring

- Many individuals modify regular clothing at home instead of purchasing adaptive wear.

- Tailors lack the expertise to make precise modifications for accessibility needs.

🗇 E-Commerce Barriers for Adaptive Clothing

- Many adaptive brands are online-only, making it hard for customers to assess fit and comfort.

- Limited return policies discourage people from experimenting with adaptive wear.

🗇 Strategies to Increase Consumer Awareness

🗇 Retail Inclusion: Making Adaptive Fashion Mainstream

- Dedicated Adaptive Fashion Sections in Stores – Large retail brands like Pantaloons, Lifestyle, and Reliance Trends should introduce in-store adaptive wear collections.

- Shop-From-Home Consultation Services – Brands should provide video consultations for accessibility needs, similar to bridal wear services.

- Trained Sales Staff in Accessibility Needs – Retail workers should understand adaptive modifications and assist customers accordingly.

🗇 E-Commerce & Online Awareness

- Better Categorization on Shopping Platforms – Adaptive clothing should have its own filter options on Myntra, Amazon, and Flipkart.

- Inclusive Advertising Campaigns – Featuring models with disabilities, elderly individuals, and sensory-sensitive users in mainstream campaigns.

- Virtual Try-On & AI-Based Size Guides – To help online shoppers find the right fit for adaptive wear.

☐ Role of Advocacy & Social Media in Promoting Adaptive Fashion

☐ Disability & Elderly Rights Organizations

- NGOs and advocacy groups can collaborate with brands to promote adaptive wear.

- Government-backed disability programs should include adaptive fashion awareness in their campaigns.

☐ Influencers & Fashion Bloggers

- Indian disability rights influencers can highlight adaptive clothing options.

- Instagram and YouTube fashion bloggers can review adaptive brands to increase visibility.

☐ Community-Driven Awareness

- Schools and workplaces can introduce adaptive dress codes for inclusivity.

- Adaptive fashion workshops can educate tailors, designers, and caregivers.

☐ Future Vision: Making Adaptive Fashion a Household Concept

- Every major retail store should have an adaptive clothing section—just like kidswear or plus-size fashion.

- Adaptive fashion should be marketed as "everyday wear" instead of just a medical necessity.

- Bridal, festival, and professional adaptive fashion must be normalized through Indian fashion weeks and media.

11.8 Adaptive Fashion in Indian Universities & Design Institutes

Fashion education plays a crucial role in shaping the future of adaptive clothing in India. However, most Indian design colleges and textile institutes still focus on mainstream fashion, ignoring the needs of people with disabilities, seniors, and individuals with mobility challenges. This section explores how fashion schools, universities, and vocational training centers can integrate adaptive fashion into their curriculums.

- Current Gaps in Fashion Education & Adaptive Design

- Lack of Formal Training in Adaptive Fashion

  - Most design programs in India do not offer courses on adaptive clothing.

  - Students are not trained in accessible fastenings, sensory-friendly fabrics, or mobility-focused cuts.

- Limited Research on Inclusive Fashion

- While sustainability and textile innovation are gaining momentum, adaptive fashion research is almost non-existent in Indian universities.

- Thesis projects rarely focus on accessibility in clothing, leading to a lack of innovation in this sector.

🗇 No Industry Collaboration for Adaptive Wear

- Top Indian design institutes (NIFT, Pearl Academy, UID, etc.) collaborate with luxury brands but rarely with hospitals, disability organizations, or geriatric care experts.

- Vocational tailoring institutes do not train tailors in adaptive modifications.

🗇 Indian Universities & Colleges That Can Lead Adaptive Fashion Innovation

🗇 NIFT (National Institute of Fashion Technology) – India's top design institute, capable of introducing adaptive fashion courses and industry partnerships.

🗇 Pearl Academy & JD Institute of Fashion Technology – Well-known for fashion innovation and trend forecasting, these institutes can research disability-inclusive clothing.

🗇 Indian Institutes of Technology (IITs) – IIT Delhi & IIT Bombay are leaders in textile technology and can integrate smart adaptive fabric research.

🗇 National Institute of Design (NID) – Specializes in human-centered design, making it ideal for developing assistive clothing technology.

- How Indian Fashion Institutes Can Integrate Adaptive Fashion

- Introducing Adaptive Fashion as a Specialization

  - Offer elective courses on accessibility in fashion for design students.

  - Train students in adaptive tailoring techniques, such as magnetic closures, elasticated fits, and wheelchair-friendly silhouettes.

- Industry Collaborations & Real-World Training

  - Partner with hospitals, disability rights groups, and senior citizen organizations to test adaptive designs.

  - Launch student-led adaptive fashion projects in collaboration with government initiatives like Skill India & Make in India.

- Research & Development in Inclusive Fashion

  - Create textile innovation labs focusing on sensory-friendly fabrics, self-adjusting clothing, and temperature-adaptive wear.

  - Encourage students to research the needs of individuals with disabilities, elderly people, and those recovering from surgeries.

- The Future of Adaptive Fashion Education in India

- Adaptive fashion should become a mainstream subject in Indian fashion and textile design courses.

- Government-backed skill development programs should train tailors & fashion entrepreneurs in adaptive modifications.

❙ Fashion institutes should collaborate with Indian adaptive wear brands to provide hands-on experience to students.

11.9 International Collaborations & Global Influence on Adaptive Fashion in India

Adaptive fashion is gaining international recognition, with global brands investing in accessible clothing innovations. India has the potential to lead in adaptive fashion manufacturing and design, but stronger collaborations with international brands, research institutions, and disability advocacy groups are needed.

❙ How International Brands Are Driving Adaptive Fashion

❙ Major Global Brands Leading Adaptive Wear

- Tommy Hilfiger Adaptive – A pioneering collection featuring magnetic closures, sensory-friendly fabrics, and wheelchair-friendly designs.

- Zappos Adaptive – An online platform offering easy-on shoes, Velcro-fastened jeans, and one-handed zipper jackets.

- Nike FlyEase – Footwear with hands-free, step-in designs, catering to individuals with limited mobility.

- Marks & Spencer Adaptive Kidswear – School uniforms with hidden elastic waistbands, Velcro shirts, and soft-seam fabrics for sensory-sensitive children.

❙ India's Role in the Global Adaptive Fashion Market

- Why India Can Become a Hub for Adaptive Clothing

    - Strong Textile Industry & Affordable Manufacturing – India is a leading exporter of cotton, silk, and handloom fabrics, making it ideal for cost-effective adaptive wear production.

    - Skilled Tailoring Workforce – Indian artisans and designers can be trained to create affordable adaptive fashion at scale.

    - Growing Demand for Affordable Adaptive Clothing – Countries like the USA, UK, Canada, and Australia need budget-friendly adaptive wear, which India can supply.

- Potential Global Partnerships for India

    - Collaborating with Western Adaptive Fashion Brands – Indian manufacturers can produce adaptive garments for international brands at lower costs.

    - Joint Research with Global Universities – Partnering with MIT, Parsons School of Design, and London College of Fashion to advance smart textiles and accessible fashion.

    - Exporting Adaptive Traditional Wear to Global Markets – Creating ready-to-wear sarees, kurta sets, and festive outfits for the Indian diaspora with disabilities.

- Successful Indo-Global Collaborations in Inclusive Fashion

- Case Study 1: Indian Textile Factories Producing Adaptive Wear for Global Brands

  - Several Indian textile mills already manufacture organic cotton and sensory-friendly fabrics used in Western adaptive brands.

  - Tamil Nadu's garment factories supply lightweight adaptive clothing for European markets.

- Case Study 2: NGO Partnerships for Disability-Inclusive Textiles

  - Indian NGOs working with disability advocacy groups have collaborated with international researchers to design low-cost adaptive uniforms for schools.

- Case Study 3: Indian Startups Entering Global Adaptive Fashion

  - Some Indian adaptive wear startups are already exporting products to overseas markets, but require better branding and outreach.

- The Future of Indo-Global Adaptive Fashion Collaborations

- Government support for international partnerships can help adaptive fashion brands scale globally.

- Indian designers should showcase adaptive collections in international fashion weeks to gain recognition.

- Exporting adaptive Indian ethnic wear can tap into the global South Asian disability community.

Chapter 12

Styling Adaptive Fashion – A Guide to Looking & Feeling Confident

Adaptive fashion isn't just about functionality—it's about feeling confident, stylish, and expressing your personality. In this chapter, we'll explore how to style adaptive outfits for different occasions, ensuring that clothing choices are both comfortable and fashionable.

12.1 Everyday Casual Styling with Adaptive Wear

Comfortable, adaptive clothing doesn't have to be boring! Here's how to create casual yet stylish looks with simple tweaks.

🗇 Easy, Effortless Outfits for Daily Wear

- Stretchable Kurta + Pull-On Pants – A comfortable cotton or jersey kurta with elastic-waist pants for all-day ease.

- Adaptive Denim + Soft Cotton Tee – Magnetic or Velcro-fly jeans paired with a tag-free, breathable t-shirt.

- Pre-Stitched Saree with Lightweight Blouse – Looks effortlessly elegant without the hassle of draping.

🗇 Quick Styling Hacks for a Polished Look

- Belt-Free, Shape-Enhancing Fits – Use elastic waistbands or structured cuts for a defined look.

- Layering with Open-Front Jackets & Shrugs – Adds instant style without restricting movement.

- Statement Jewelry That's Easy to Wear – Opt for magnetic bracelets, clip-on earrings, and slip-on bangles.

12.2 Dressing Up for Work & Professional Settings

❐ Office-Ready Adaptive Wear

- Magnetic-Closure Button-Down Shirt + Stretchable Pants – A formal yet adaptive combo.

- Front-Zip Tunic + Straight Pants – Looks professional without tight collars or complex fastenings.

- Smart Blazer with Hidden Velcro Closures – A tailored look without struggling with buttons.

❐ Quick Office Styling Tips

- Stick to Classic Colors – Neutral shades like navy, grey, and pastels create a polished look.

- Adaptive Loafers & Slip-On Formal Shoes – No laces, no hassle—just sleek comfort.

- Structured Bags with Easy Closures – Use magnetic-flap handbags for accessibility.

12.3 Festive & Wedding Styling with Adaptive Fashion

Traditional Indian wear can be modified for ease without losing elegance.

🗇 Effortless Festive Outfits

- Pre-Draped Saree with Clip-On Pallu – Securely fastened for a perfect drape without pleating.

- Side-Zip Lehengas with Stretchable Blouses – Easy-to-wear ethnic wear that allows movement.

- Sherwanis & Kurtas with Velcro Closures – Traditional, yet easy to put on without small buttons.

🗇 Quick Festive Styling Hacks

- Use Dupatta Clips for Secure Draping – No constant adjusting required.

- Soft, Non-Slip Juttis & Kolhapuris – Adaptive traditional footwear for all-day comfort.

- Minimal Jewelry That Makes a Statement – Lightweight, easy-to-wear pieces that don't irritate the skin.

12.4 Styling Adaptive Fashion for Special Occasions

Looking good at a party, dinner, or celebration while staying comfortable is possible!

⏹ Glam Looks Without the Hassle

- One-Piece Adaptive Jumpsuits – Dressy, yet easy to wear with side zippers or elastic backs.

- Front-Opening Evening Gowns – Elegant designs with hidden magnetic or Velcro closures.

- Smart Wrap Dresses & Tunics – Flattering and adjustable to body changes.

⏹ Confidence-Boosting Styling Tips

- Choose Fabrics That Flow & Flatter – Soft silks, georgettes, and stretch cottons enhance movement.

- Go for Pre-Stitched Drape Elements – Looks stylish without effort.

- Add Stylish Layering for a Chic Touch – Open shrugs, lightweight stoles, or ponchos.

⏹ Final Takeaway: Adaptive fashion is about style, comfort, and self-expression. No matter the occasion, feeling good in what you wear makes all the difference!

12.5 Celebrity & Real-Life Inspirations for Adaptive Fashion

Fashion is about self-expression, and many public figures have embraced adaptive wear to suit their needs. Whether it's celebrities, influencers, or everyday style icons, adaptive fashion can be bold, stylish, and empowering.

- Celebrity Icons Who Champion Adaptive Fashion

- Deepika Padukone – Comfort-First Elegance

The Bollywood queen often prioritizes comfortable silhouettes with structured elegance.

- Pre-Draped Sarees – Her love for fluid, fuss-free sarees is perfect for adaptive wear.

- Relaxed-Fit Blazers & Wide-Leg Trousers – Stylish yet easy for movement.

- Minimal Jewelry & Classic Hairstyles – Effortless styling without overcomplication.

- Sonam Kapoor – Fusion & Functional Fashion

Known for her experimental style, Sonam Kapoor proves that fashion can be both bold and accessible.

- Front-Zip Anarkalis & Jackets – Traditional, yet mobility-friendly.

- Slip-On Kolhapuris & Sneakers with Sarees – Stylish and practical for long wear.

- Statement Layers Like Ponchos & Capes – Adds drama without tight-fitting garments.

- Ayushmann Khurrana – Effortless Adaptive Menswear

Ayushmann often chooses relaxed, yet structured pieces that work well for adaptive dressing.

- Elastic-Waist Trousers in Luxe Fabrics – Comfortable without looking casual.

- Sherwanis with Side Zippers Instead of Buttons – Traditional yet functional.

- Slip-On Mojaris & Loafers – Eliminates bending or adjusting hassle.

❒ Real-Life Style Icons Who Inspire Adaptive Fashion

❒ Sinéad Burke – Disability Advocate & Fashion Influencer

Sinéad Burke, an international disability activist, works with Gucci, Burberry, and Vogue to promote adaptive fashion.

- Custom-Tailored Dresses with Side Openings – Easy to wear without compromising on elegance.
- Velcro Fastened Coats for Winter Styling – Fashionable without restrictive closures.

❒ Aarifah Rebello – Indian Musician & Adaptive Style Star

Mumbai-based musician Aarifah Rebello embraces gender-neutral, loose-fitted styles that can easily be adapted for accessibility.

- Oversized Cotton Shirts & Elastic Joggers – Stylish yet mobility-friendly.
- Sneakers with Adaptive Laces – No-fuss streetwear inspiration.

❒ How to Adapt Celebrity & Influencer Styles for Everyday Wear

❒ Love a celebrity's outfit? Here's how to make it adaptive!

- Swap zippers for Velcro or magnets – Blazers, kurtas, and dresses can look exactly the same but be easier to wear.

- Use stretch panels & elastic waistbands – Keeps the look sleek while adding comfort.

- Choose lightweight, breathable fabrics – Bollywood loves silk and brocade, but opt for cotton blends for ease.

- Replace high heels with stylish flats – Embellished juttis, sneakers, or adaptive footwear can elevate any outfit.

🗇 Final Takeaway: Fashion isn't just about trends—it's about finding styles that make you feel your best. Whether it's Bollywood glamour or everyday elegance, adaptive fashion can be just as chic, expressive, and confidence-boosting!

12.6 DIY Styling Tips for Different Body Types & Comfort Preferences

Adaptive fashion isn't just about accessibility—it's about flattering your body shape while ensuring maximum comfort. No matter your body type, there are ways to style outfits that highlight your best features while accommodating mobility or sensory needs.

🗇 Dressing for Different Body Types with Adaptive Fashion

🗇 Apple Shape (Weight Around Midsection, Slimmer Legs & Arms)

- Go for Flowy Kurtas & Tunics – Avoid tight-fitting tops; opt for A-line silhouettes that don't cling.

- Elastic-Waist, Straight-Leg Pants – Provides a structured yet comfortable look.

- Draped Jackets or Open Shrugs – Adds layers without bulk.

🗗 Adaptive Hacks:

- Avoid Buttons & Zippers at the Midsection – Choose side-open kurtas or magnetic closures.

- Structured Shoulder or Collar Details – Draws attention upward, balancing proportions.

🗗 Pear Shape (Wider Hips, Narrower Shoulders & Waist)

- Structured Tops & Jackets – Adds balance to the upper body.

- Flared or Palazzo Pants with Soft Elastic Waistbands – Flatters curves without being restrictive.

- Pre-Pleated Sarees or Wrap Dresses – Highlights the waist without emphasizing the hips.

🗗 Adaptive Hacks:

- Soft-Fabric Dupattas or Scarves Instead of Heavy Layers – Avoids adding bulk around the lower body.

- Velcro or Stretchable Saree Petticoats – Allows movement without discomfort.

🗐 Styling Tips for Individuals with Sensory Sensitivities

- Avoid Heavy Seams & Rough Fabrics – Choose cotton, modal, or bamboo fabrics.

- Go for Tag-Free, Soft-Lined Clothing – No scratchy labels.

- Use Stretch Panels Instead of Zippers – Easier dressing without rigid fastenings.

🗐 Styling for Limited Mobility or Seated Positions

- Higher Waistbands on Pants & Skirts – Ensures clothing stays in place when sitting.

- Shorter Hemlines in the Front, Longer in the Back – Prevents fabric from bunching.

- Front-Opening Kurtas & Shirts – No lifting arms to wear tops.

🗐 Adaptive Hacks:

- Side-Opening Palazzo Pants for Wheelchair Users – Makes dressing easier.

- Stretch-Panel Sherwanis & Blazers – Keeps traditional wear comfortable for longer periods.

🗐 **Final Takeaway: Adaptive styling isn't about hiding your body**—it's about enhancing comfort while embracing confidence. The right cuts, fabrics, and small modifications can transform any outfit into a fashion-forward, accessible look!

Chapter 13

Building a Functional & Stylish Adaptive Wardrobe

Creating a versatile, adaptive wardrobe doesn't mean giving up on style. A well-planned closet should have comfortable staples, easy-to-wear statement pieces, and adaptable options for any occasion. This chapter helps you curate a wardrobe that's practical, fashionable, and suited to your personal needs.

13.1 The Essentials of an Adaptive Wardrobe

Before buying or modifying clothes, focus on key wardrobe essentials that ensure:

- Comfort & Ease of Dressing – No complex fastenings or tight fits.
- Flexibility for Different Occasions – Staples that can be dressed up or down.
- Low-Maintenance Fabrics – Wrinkle-free, stretchable, and breathable.

🗐 Must-Have Adaptive Clothing Pieces

🗐 Everyday Basics

- Tag-Free, Stretchable Tees & Kurtas – For daily comfort.
- Elastic-Waist Trousers & Palazzo Pants – No zippers, just slip-on ease.

- Front-Zip or Magnetic-Closure Jackets – Stylish yet effortless to wear.

🗇 Semi-Formal & Workwear

- Smart-Casual Blouses & Tunics with Side Openings – Keeps dressing quick & easy.

- Stretchable Formal Trousers with Concealed Elastic – Ensures a polished yet comfortable fit.

- Velcro or Snap-Button Blazers – Professional without fussing over buttons.

🗇 Special Occasion Wear

- Pre-Draped Sarees & Anarkalis with Adjustable Closures – Traditional without complications.

- Sherwanis & Jackets with Hidden Zippers – Looks formal but easier to wear.

- Adaptive Ethnic Footwear – Slip-on mojaris, juttis, and chappals with adjustable straps.

🗇 Seasonal Must-Haves

- Breathable Cotton & Linen for Summer – Keeps cool and comfortable.

- Lightweight Wool or Fleece for Winter – Warm without heavy layers.

- Easy-Wear Raincoats & Non-Slip Footwear for Monsoons – Functional yet stylish.

13.2 Smart Shopping Tips for Adaptive Clothing

When buying new pieces, look for:

- Hidden Adaptive Features in Regular Clothing – Elastic waistbands, stretch panels, wide necklines.

- Easy-to-Care Fabrics – Machine-washable, wrinkle-resistant materials.

- Multi-Use Pieces – A kurta that doubles as a dress, or a blazer that works for both casual and formal settings.

🗗 Where to Shop for Adaptive Clothing in India:

- Department Stores – Some brands now offer pull-on styles & elasticated fits.

- Boutiques & Tailors – Custom alterations for adaptive needs.

- Online Platforms – Look for adaptive sections on Myntra, Ajio, and Amazon India.

13.3 Capsule Wardrobe: Fewer Clothes, More Styling Options

A capsule wardrobe helps reduce clutter while ensuring maximum outfit combinations. The idea is to own versatile pieces that mix and match effortlessly.

🗗 How to Build an Adaptive Capsule Wardrobe

- Choose a Neutral Base – Whites, beiges, greys, pastels – easy to pair with anything.

- Add Statement Pieces – A bright stole, embroidered kurta, or a printed blazer adds flair.

- Invest in Multi-Way Clothing – A dress that converts into a kurta, or a poncho that doubles as a jacket.

🗇   Final Takeaway:

A well-thought-out adaptive wardrobe saves time, reduces stress, and keeps you looking stylish effortlessly. Focus on comfort, versatility, and ease of wear, and you'll never feel like you have 'nothing to wear' again!

Chapter 14

Adaptive Fashion & Personal Identity – Expressing Yourself Through Style

Fashion is more than just clothing—it's a reflection of personality, confidence, and individuality. Adaptive fashion doesn't mean compromising on self-expression. This chapter explores how to use color, patterns, accessories, and personal styling to celebrate your unique identity while prioritizing comfort and accessibility.

14.1 The Psychology of Fashion: How Clothes Affect Confidence

What we wear influences:

- Mood & Energy Levels – Bright colors = uplifting, dark tones = sophisticated.

- Body Language & Social Perception – Well-fitted outfits make you feel more confident in social settings.

- Comfort = Confidence – If something feels good to wear, it automatically boosts self-assurance.

🗇 Key Tip: Choose clothing that makes you feel empowered, unrestricted, and authentically YOU.

14.2 Finding Your Personal Style in Adaptive Fashion

Your personal style should reflect your:

- Lifestyle – Do you prefer casual comfort, elegant minimalism, or bold statement pieces?

- Cultural Identity – How can you adapt traditional wear while keeping it accessible?

- Sensory Preferences – Do you love soft fabrics, loose fits, or structured silhouettes?

🗇 Style Quiz: Which Adaptive Fashion Persona Are You?

The Minimalist: Prefers neutral colors, clean cuts, and effortless styling.

The Trendsetter: Loves bold prints, unique cuts, and fashion-forward looks.

The Comfort Lover: Prioritizes loose fits, soft fabrics, and breathable layers.

The Ethnic Chic: Mixes traditional elements with modern adaptive features.

14.3 Using Color & Patterns to Make a Statement

🗇 Understanding Color Psychology

- Pastels & Neutrals – Calm, elegant, and versatile.

- Bold & Bright Colors – Energetic, confident, and eye-catching.

- Monochrome Looks – Chic, polished, and easy to coordinate.

🗇 Tip: If you want a pop of color, choose bright scarves, statement jewelry, or embroidered details.

14.4 Accessorizing for Personal Expression

Accessories can instantly elevate any adaptive outfit.

- Magnetic or Clip-On Jewelry – Stylish without tricky clasps.

- Scarves & Dupattas with Pre-Sewn Pleats – Adds a fashionable touch without frequent adjustments.

- Statement Shoes with Adaptive Comfort – Embellished slip-ons, customized sneakers, or flexible juttis.

- Tip: Play with textures, metallics, and soft embellishments to add personality without compromising comfort.

- Final Takeaway: Fashion should always make you feel authentic, empowered, and comfortable. Whether you love minimalist elegance or bold statements, adaptive fashion is not about limitations—it's about possibilities!

14.5 Real-Life Adaptive Style Transformations

Fashion can be life-changing when it truly meets personal needs. Here are inspiring real-life transformations where adaptive clothing allowed people to regain confidence, independence, and self-expression.

- Case Study 1: Rekha's Saree Transformation

- Challenge: Rekha, 55, loved wearing sarees but found draping difficult after developing arthritis.

- Adaptive Solution: She switched to pre-draped sarees with a side zipper and magnetic blouses, allowing her to dress independently.

- Style Impact: Rekha no longer needed help to get ready and felt elegant at family gatherings again.

- Case Study 2: Arjun's Sherwani Upgrade

- Challenge: Arjun, 29, wanted to wear a sherwani to his wedding but struggled with fine motor coordination due to a past injury.

- Adaptive Solution: His tailor added hidden Velcro closures inside the sherwani and elastic churidar pants instead of a drawstring.

- Style Impact: Arjun felt confident and independent on his big day, without struggling with fastenings.

- Case Study 3: Priya's Workwear Reinvention

- Challenge: Priya, 38, worked in corporate finance but found tight formal wear restrictive due to sensory sensitivities.

- Adaptive Solution: She switched to soft, stretch-fabric trousers with side zippers and button-free blazers with magnetic fastenings.

- Style Impact: Priya now walks into meetings feeling comfortable and stylish, without distractions from fabric discomfort.

- Case Study 4: Kabir's Everyday Footwear Fix

- Challenge: Kabir, 19, had a mobility condition that made traditional lace-up sneakers difficult.

- ◫ Adaptive Solution: He replaced shoelaces with elastic, slip-on bands and added extra padding for support.

- ◫ Style Impact: Kabir now wears fashionable sneakers that fit his lifestyle, without needing help to tie them.

- ◫ The Power of Adaptive Style

Adaptive fashion doesn't take away from personal expression—it enhances it. The right modifications can bring back:

- Confidence – Feeling good in what you wear.

- Independence – Dressing without extra assistance.

- Style Freedom – Wearing the outfits you love, without limitations.

14.6 DIY Before-and-After Styling Tips for Adaptive Fashion

A few small modifications can turn a frustrating outfit into a stylish, functional look. Here are easy before-and-after DIY tips to transform everyday wear into adaptive, confidence-boosting fashion.

- ◫ 1. Saree & Lehenga Transformation

- ◫ Before:

- ◫ Heavy pleats, difficult to drape.

- ◫ Blouse hooks at the back, hard to fasten.

- ◫ Petticoat drawstrings need adjusting.

- After (Adaptive Fixes):
  - Pre-stitched saree with elastic waistband – Just step in and go!
  - Side-zip or magnetic-closure blouse – No more struggling with back hooks.
  - Adjustable, stretchable petticoat – Sits comfortably without tying strings.
- Result: Looks just as elegant, but dressing takes seconds instead of minutes!
- 2. Workwear Shirt & Blazer Makeover
- Before:
- Tight button-up shirts, difficult to fasten.
- Stiff, restrictive blazers.
- Formal trousers with tricky zippers.
- After (Adaptive Fixes):
  - Magnetic or Velcro-front shirts – Same formal look, zero effort to button up.
  - Blazer with hidden stretch panels – Allows movement without stiffness.
  - Side-zip or elastic-waist trousers – Looks tailored, but feels like loungewear.
- Result: You still look polished, but dressing is effortless!
- 3. Jeans & Everyday Bottoms Upgrade
- Before:
- Button-fly jeans are hard to close.

- Skinny jeans restrict movement.
- Churidar drawstrings get tangled.
- After (Adaptive Fixes):
  - Elasticated waistband jeans with faux buttons – Same look, easy pull-on style.
  - Straight-leg stretch denim – Moves with you instead of against you.
  - Churidars with hidden side zippers – Traditional yet quick to wear.
- Result: Everyday pants that look stylish without the struggle!
- 4. Footwear Fix for Style & Comfort
- Before:
- Formal shoes require lacing up.
- Heels are painful for long wear.
- Traditional juttis lack flexibility.
- After (Adaptive Fixes):
  - Slip-on formal loafers with hidden stretch – No laces, just step in!
  - Block heels or wedge footwear – Stylish but more stable than stilettos.
  - Adaptive juttis with soft padding – Keeps the look authentic but pain-free.
- Result: Stylish shoes that feel like walking on clouds!
- Final Takeaway:

Adaptive fashion doesn't mean giving up on personal style—it just means finding creative, easy-to-wear solutions that make dressing effortless while keeping you looking your best!

14.7 Styling Adaptive Fashion for Different Age Groups

Fashion should be adaptive at every stage of life, evolving with changing needs while maintaining personal style. Here's how to style comfortable, functional, and trendy outfits for different age groups.

◻ Teens & Young Adults: Fashion Meets Functionality

Teenagers and young adults want trendy, expressive styles but also need clothing that's comfortable, adaptable, and easy to manage.

- Streetwear Meets Adaptive Wear – Loose-fit joggers with elastic waistbands, zip-up hoodies, and pull-on sneakers.

- College & Work-Ready Styles – Magnetic-button shirts, stretchable jeans, and trendy yet easy-fasten footwear.

- Adaptive Partywear – Wrap dresses, adjustable lehengas, or stretch sherwanis with hidden zippers.

◻ Styling Tip: Go for layered looks, oversized fits, and easy-wear sneakers for an effortlessly cool vibe.

◻ Adults: Balancing Style & Comfort

Most adults juggle work, social life, and family responsibilities, so adaptive clothing should be practical yet stylish.

- Workwear Redefined – Blazers with magnetic closures, side-zip formal pants, and tag-free, soft shirts.

- Fusion Wear for Outings – Pre-stitched sarees, stretch churidars, and modern Indo-Western tunics.

- Adaptive Evening Wear – Sleek wrap jumpsuits, pre-draped gowns, and Velcro-fastened Nehru jackets.

🗇 Styling Tip: Stick to neutral, classic colors for versatile outfits that transition from work to social events effortlessly.

🗇 Seniors: Timeless Comfort & Ease of Dressing

For seniors, ease of movement and soft, breathable fabrics are key, while still maintaining a refined, elegant look.

- Adaptive Sarees & Kurtas – Front-open button-free kurtas, lightweight pre-draped sarees, and stretchable blouses.

- Easy-Access Footwear – Non-slip, Velcro-fastened sandals and cushioned formal wear.

- Layering for Comfort – Soft shawls, ponchos, and zip-front sweaters instead of complex fastenings.

🗇 Styling Tip: Choose lightweight, flowy fabrics that provide movement without restriction.

🗇 Final Takeaway:

No matter your age, fashion should be about confidence, personal expression, and ease. Whether you're dressing for school, work, or special occasions, adaptive styling ensures fashion is truly for everyone!

14.8 Cultural & Regional Adaptations in Adaptive Fashion

India's diverse culture means that fashion isn't just about personal style—it's deeply connected to tradition, festivals, and regional identity. Adaptive fashion should allow people to wear culturally significant attire without compromising comfort or ease of dressing.

🗇 North India: Adaptive Festive & Wedding Wear

In Punjab, Delhi, Rajasthan, and Uttar Pradesh, traditional clothing like lehengas, sherwanis, and heavy dupattas are common for celebrations.

- Pre-Stitched Lehengas with Elastic Waistbands – No need for drawstrings or tight zippers.

- Sherwanis with Hidden Velcro Closures – Same royal look, but easy to wear without buttons.

- Clip-On Turbans & Pre-Tied Pagris – Perfect for Sikh men who prefer ready-to-wear styles.

🗇 Hack: Use lightweight silk or georgette instead of heavy brocades for ease of movement.

🗇 South India: Adaptive Sarees & Traditional Wear

Southern Indian styles often feature silk sarees, veshtis (dhotis), and Kanjeevaram blouses, which can be adapted for accessibility.

- Pre-Draped Silk Sarees with Side-Zip Pallus – Maintains authentic drape without pleating hassle.

- Elastic-Waist Veshtis (Dhotis) with Side Slits – Allows quick wear while keeping the traditional silhouette.

- Magnetic-Closure Kanjeevaram Blouses – No need for back hooks or tight buttons.

🗗 Hack: Use cotton-silk blends instead of heavy silk for breathability and flexibility.

🗗 West India: Adaptive Gujarati & Maharashtrian Styles

Gujarati and Maharashtrian attire includes bandhani sarees, Navari sarees, kediyu jackets, and dhotis, which can be made more functional for everyday wear.

- Pre-Pleated Navari Sarees with Adjustable Straps – No need to wrap and pin.

- Velcro Kediyu Jackets – Traditional yet quick to fasten.

- Side-Zip Embroidered Dhotis – Keeps the draped look intact but adds ease of wear.

🗗 Hack: Use hidden stretch panels in blouses and jackets for mobility-friendly outfits.

🗗 East India: Adaptive Bengali, Assamese & Odia Attire

Traditional Bengali sarees, Assamese Mekhela Chador, and Odia Sambalpuri drapes can be modified for accessibility.

- Bengali Sarees with Pre-Sewn Pleats – Easy-to-wear without pinning the pallu.
- Elastic Mekhela Chadors – Allows for adjustable fit without complex wrapping.
- Soft Cotton Dhutis with Side Openings – Perfect for elderly wearers or individuals with mobility needs.

🗇 Hack: Add button-free blouses with side zippers for quick dressing.

🗇 Adaptive Clothing for Religious & Spiritual Practices

- Pre-Tied Dupattas for Gurdwara Visits – No need for constant adjusting.
- Slip-On Kurtas for Temple Visits – Traditional but without tight collars.
- Easy-Drape Hajibs & Abayas – Magnetic or Velcro closures for quick wear.

🗇 Hack: Opt for moisture-wicking, breathable fabrics for long religious ceremonies.

🗇 Final Takeaway:

Adaptive fashion should embrace cultural identity while making traditional wear accessible for all. No one should have to give up their heritage because of clothing limitations!

Chapter 15

The Business of Adaptive Fashion – Opportunities & Challenges

Adaptive fashion is not just a social movement; it's a growing industry with massive market potential. This chapter explores business opportunities, consumer demand, and the challenges faced by designers and brands in making adaptive fashion mainstream.

15.1 Why Adaptive Fashion is a Booming Industry

The demand for accessible, stylish clothing is increasing due to:

- Aging Populations – More seniors need easy-wear clothing.

- Increased Disability Awareness – Better representation is driving market demand.

- Rise of Comfort-First Fashion – More people prioritize ease over trends.

- Technology-Enabled Fashion – Smart textiles, AI sizing, and 3D printing are making adaptive clothing more customizable.

🗗 Market Insight: The global adaptive fashion industry is expected to grow to $400 billion+ by 2030.

15.2 Business Opportunities in Adaptive Fashion

🗇 Retail & E-Commerce Brands

- Creating Adaptive Clothing Lines in Existing Brands – Brands like Fabindia, Biba, Manyavar can integrate adaptive features into their collections.

- Specialized Online Marketplaces – A platform like Myntra Adaptive could cater specifically to Indian adaptive wear.

🗇 Boutique & Custom Tailoring

- Luxury Adaptive Fashion – High-end labels can create customized, stylish adaptive wear.

- Traditional Indian Wear for Accessibility – Boutiques can offer pre-stitched sarees, sherwanis with easy closures, and wheelchair-friendly lehengas.

🗇 Smart & Tech-Enabled Adaptive Fashion

- AI-Based Custom Tailoring – Virtual body scanning for personalized fits.

- Temperature-Regulating Fabrics – Ideal for people with sensory sensitivities.

15.3 Challenges in the Adaptive Fashion Industry

🗇 Limited Awareness & Representation

- Most retailers don't consider adaptive fashion a mainstream category.

- Lack of visibility in fashion weeks, influencer marketing, and Bollywood.

🗇 High Production Costs

- Magnetic closures, seamless stitching, and custom tailoring increase prices.
- Adaptive wear is often seen as 'specialized' rather than mainstream.

🗇 Lack of Standard Sizing

- Indian body types vary widely, making universal adaptive sizing difficult.
- Brands must develop flexible, adjustable sizing systems.

🗇 The Future: How to Make Adaptive Fashion More Profitable & Scalable

- Government support & tax benefits for adaptive brands.
- Retail collaborations with mainstream brands.
- More influencer and celebrity endorsements.
- Exporting adaptive Indian fashion globally.

15.4 How to Start an Adaptive Fashion Brand

For entrepreneurs looking to break into the adaptive fashion industry, the key is to combine style with accessibility while keeping production costs sustainable. This section provides a step-by-step guide to launching a successful adaptive fashion brand.

Step 1: Identify Your Niche in Adaptive Fashion

Not all adaptive clothing brands are the same. Choose a specific category to specialize in:

- Traditional Adaptive Wear – Pre-stitched sarees, Velcro sherwanis, accessible lehengas.

- Workwear & Formal Clothing – Magnetic-closure shirts, stretchable suits.

- Casual Everyday Wear – Easy-fastening jeans, pull-on kurtas, seamless activewear.

- Footwear & Accessories – Adaptive mojaris, clip-on dupattas, one-hand belts.

🗇 Pro Tip: Find a gap in the market—for example, there are very few affordable adaptive ethnic brands in India.

Step 2: Design for Accessibility & Style

Your designs should be both functional and fashionable. Consider:

- Easy Fastenings – Velcro, magnetic buttons, stretchable necklines.

- Sensory-Friendly Fabrics – Soft cotton, bamboo, seamless linings.

- Adjustable Fits – Elastic panels, drawstring waistbands, side zippers.

- Stylish Adaptations – Pre-pleated sarees, tuxedo shirts with hidden closures.

🗇 Tip: Partner with tailors, physical therapists, or disability advocates to test your designs.

Step 3: Source the Right Materials & Manufacturers

- Find Suppliers Who Offer Adaptive Fabrics – Soft, breathable, and stretchable materials.

- Work with Skilled Tailors – Train them in adaptive modifications.

- Look for Ethical Manufacturing Units – Prefer local, small-scale artisans to keep costs low.

Tip: Many Indian handloom clusters (like Khadi Weavers) are looking to innovate—this is a great opportunity for collaboration.

Step 4: Build Your Brand Identity & Online Presence

- Create a Strong Brand Story – Adaptive fashion is not just a product, it's a movement.

- Use Social Media to Educate & Promote – Partner with influencers who advocate for disability rights.

- Launch a User-Friendly E-Commerce Store – Ensure the website is accessible (voice navigation, easy checkout, flexible return policies).

Tip: Highlight real customer stories to showcase the impact of adaptive fashion.

Step 5: Pricing, Marketing & Selling Adaptive Wear

- Offer Affordable Yet Profitable Pricing – Adaptive fashion should be accessible, not overly expensive.

- Sell Through Multiple Channels – Website, social media, Amazon India, niche fashion marketplaces.

- Collaborate with Retailers – Pitch adaptive collections to Fabindia, Biba, Lifestyle, and handicraft stores.

🗇 Tip: Government grants & startup incubators support businesses in inclusive fashion—apply for funding!

🗇 Final Takeaway:

Starting an adaptive fashion brand is not just a business—it's a revolution in inclusive style. By focusing on comfort, dignity, and accessibility, entrepreneurs can create meaningful impact while building a profitable business.

Chapter 16

Adaptive Fashion Hacks
You Can Try Today

You don't need to buy new clothes to make your wardrobe adaptive and accessible. With a few DIY tricks, you can modify your favorite outfits to be easier to wear, more comfortable, and stylish.

16.1 Quick Fixes for Common Clothing Problems

- Struggling with Tight Collars & Necklines?

    - Hack: Use a seam ripper to loosen the collar seam slightly for extra stretch.

    - Alternative: Attach a small hidden elastic loop to the button for flexibility.

- Buttons Are Hard to Fasten?

    - Hack: Replace buttons with stick-on Velcro or magnetic closures behind the button strip.

    - Alternative: Use decorative snap buttons that look stylish but fasten instantly.

- Pants Too Tight Around the Waist?

    - Hack: Sew a stretchable fabric panel into the sides or back for flexibility.

    - Alternative: Use a hair tie looped around the button to expand the waistband without sewing.

- ⬚ Dupattas or Scarves Keep Slipping?
    - Hack: Sew small snap buttons onto your shoulders and dupatta corners to keep it in place.
    - Alternative: Use lightweight fashion tape to secure it without damaging fabric.

16.2 No – Sew Adaptive Clothing Hacks

- ⬚ Convert a T-Shirt into an Easy-Wear Top
    - Hack: Cut the back into two panels and attach Velcro strips for a no-pull dressing option.
- ⬚ Turn Jeans into Elastic-Waist Pants
    - Hack: Remove the zipper, replace it with an elastic band inside the waistband, and sew it shut.
- ⬚ Make Any Dress or Kurta Front-Opening
    - Hack: Use iron-on Velcro strips along the center seam, keeping the design intact.
- ⬚ Adaptive Shoes Without Buying New Ones
    - Hack: Replace laces with elastic shoelaces or sew in a side zipper for easy access.

16.3 Hacks for Dressing Faster & Easier

- Layer Clothes the Smart Way – Wear magnetic closure shirts under jackets, so you don't struggle with layers.
- Use a Dressing Hook or Button Hook – Helps fasten small buttons with one hand.

- Pre-Fasten Belts & Jewelry – Use magnetic belt buckles & clip-on jewelry to avoid fumbling.

🗇 Bonus Hack: Use baby powder to slide into tight sleeves or pants smoothly!

🗇 Final Takeaway:

Adaptive fashion doesn't have to be expensive or complicated. With a few simple modifications, you can make any outfit work for you—without sacrificing style!

16.4 Adaptive Fashion Hacks for Specific Needs

Everyone has unique dressing challenges, whether it's due to mobility limitations, recovery after surgery, or the need for wheelchair-friendly clothing. Here are some simple but effective DIY modifications to make dressing easier for specific needs.

🗇 Post-Surgery & Medical Dressing Hacks

After surgery, clothing should be easy to wear, non-restrictive, and gentle on the skin.

- Hack: Convert any T-shirt or kurta into a front-opening top using Velcro or snap buttons.

- Hack: Attach fabric loops to sleeves and pant legs to help with dressing without lifting arms or legs.

- Hack: Sew in hidden zippers or side openings for easy access to IV lines, bandages, or casts.

- Hack: Use wrap-around skirts or lungis instead of tight pants for lower-body surgery recovery.

🗇 Bonus Tip: Choose moisture-wicking fabrics to avoid irritation around stitches or sensitive skin.

🗇 Wheelchair-Friendly Clothing Hacks

Sitting for long hours means clothes should be comfortable, non-bulky, and not ride up.

- Hack: Use elastic waistbands with a higher back and lower front for pants that fit well when sitting.

- Hack: Replace traditional zippers with side-open closures or magnetic buttons for easy dressing.

- Hack: Sew anti-slip fabric or silicone grips on the back of clothes to prevent sliding.

- Hack: Shorten the front hem of jackets & shirts so they don't bunch up while seated.

🗇 Bonus Tip: Layer poncho-style sweaters or capes instead of tight jackets for easy wear.

🗇 Adaptive Hacks for Arthritis or Limited Hand Mobility

- Hack: Use looped zipper pulls or attach a keyring to zippers for an easier grip.

- Hack: Replace small shirt buttons with snap closures or larger, easy-grip buttons.

- Hack: Choose pull-on skirts and pants instead of hook-and-eye closures.

- Hack: Opt for stretchable bracelets and clip-on accessories instead of traditional jewelry.

❏ Bonus Tip: Use foam tubing around brush handles, belts, and bag straps for better grip.

❏ Final Takeaway:

Adaptive fashion should be about convenience, not compromise. A few small changes can make a huge difference in comfort, independence, and confidence!

16.5 Adaptive Fashion Hacks for Extreme Weather

Dressing comfortably in harsh summers, chilly winters, and unpredictable monsoons can be challenging, especially when mobility, sensory, or health factors come into play. Here's how to modify clothing for year-round comfort without sacrificing style.

❏ Hot Summers: Stay Cool & Sweat-Free

- Hack: Sew hidden mesh panels under arms and on the back of shirts to allow airflow.

- Hack: Convert heavy dupattas or stoles into lightweight, moisture-wicking fabric like cotton voile.

- Hack: Use loose, airy tunics with side openings instead of tight-fitted kurtas.

- Hack: Attach Velcro straps on the sides of long skirts or saris to allow easy movement.

- Hack: Switch to magnetic-closure sandals instead of buckled or lace-up shoes for quick removal.

🗇 Bonus Tip: Wear light-colored, UV-protective fabrics to reflect heat.

❄ **Cold Winters: Stay Warm Without Bulk**

- Hack: Use zip-up fleece ponchos or shrugs instead of heavy sweaters for easier dressing.

- Hack: Sew fingerless gloves into coat sleeves to keep hands warm without losing dexterity.

- Hack: Convert normal socks into compression socks by adding soft elastic bands to prevent swelling.

- Hack: Choose front-open woolen layers instead of pullovers to avoid struggle with tight necklines.

- Hack: Attach hidden fasteners inside shawls to prevent slipping off shoulders.

🗇 Bonus Tip: Opt for thermo-lined leggings instead of tight-fitted wool pants for warmth without restriction.

🗇 Rainy Monsoon Season: Stay Dry & Comfortable

- Hack: Waterproof regular sneakers by spraying them with a clear, water-repellent spray.

- Hack: Replace drawstring hoods on raincoats with elastic-fitted caps for easy wear.

- Hack: Use quick-dry, stretch fabrics like polyester-cotton blends to prevent soggy, heavy clothing.

- Hack: Convert normal jeans into waterproof monsoon pants by applying beeswax or a fabric sealant.

- Hack: Attach Velcro straps to raincoats instead of zippers for quick dressing.

🗗 Bonus Tip: Use clip-on waterproof shoe covers instead of struggling with bulky rain boots.

🗗 Final Takeaway:

Weather shouldn't be a barrier to style or comfort. With small modifications, you can dress smartly for any season without hassle !

Chapter 17

Breaking Fashion Myths – Adaptive Clothing Can Be Trendy Too!

Many people assume that adaptive fashion is plain, dull, or only for medical needs—but that's far from the truth! This chapter debunks common myths and proves that style and accessibility can go hand in hand.

17.1 Myth #1: Adaptive Clothing Looks Like Hospital Wear

- False! Adaptive fashion today includes:

    - Chic pre-stitched sarees & lehengas – No draping struggle, just slip on and go!

    - Modern, structured blazers with hidden Velcro – Business-ready but effortless.

    - Stylish elastic-waist jeans & kurta sets – Tailored, not baggy!

- Reality Check: Brands like Tommy Hilfiger Adaptive & Zappos Adaptive prove that accessible fashion can be runway-worthy.

17.2 Myth #2: You Have to Sacrifice Trends for Comfort

- False! Adaptive fashion can be:

    - Inspired by Bollywood trends – Magnetic-button sherwanis, sarees with built-in pleats.

- Street-style ready – Slip-on sneakers, oversized graphic tees with adaptive fastenings.
- Red-carpet worthy – Front-zip gowns, pre-draped Indo-Western outfits.

Reality Check: Style icons like Deepika Padukone, Sonam Kapoor, and Priyanka Chopra often wear loose, comfortable silhouettes that work great for adaptive wear too!

17.3 Myth #3: Adaptive Footwear is Unfashionable

False! Modern adaptive footwear includes:

- Slip-on juttis with hidden elastic – No buckles, all elegance.
- Stylish sneakers with no-tie laces – Effortless and trendy.
- Adaptive heels with secure straps – Chic yet easy to wear.

Reality Check: You can turn ANY stylish shoe into an adaptive one by swapping laces for elastic bands or adding side zippers.

17.4 Myth #4: Only People with Disabilities Wear Adaptive Fashion

False! Adaptive fashion benefits:

- Pregnant women – Stretchable waistbands, easy-fasten tops.

- Seniors – Clothes that prioritize ease and dignity.
- Travelers – Wrinkle-free, quick-dressing styles.

🗗 Reality Check: Fashion is for everyone—adaptive clothing just makes it more inclusive.

17.5 Myth #5: Adaptive Clothing is Always Expensive

🗗 False! Budget-friendly options exist:

- DIY modifications – Convert regular clothes into adaptive wear at home.

- Affordable adaptive brands – Many local tailors can create custom adaptive pieces at lower costs.

- Smart shopping – Buy ready-made stretchable, magnetic, or elasticated clothing from mainstream brands.

🗗 Reality Check: Style is about how you wear it, not how much you spend!

🗗 Final Takeaway:

Adaptive fashion isn't about limitations—it's about breaking barriers and redefining style! You don't have to choose between fashion and function when you can have both.

17.6 Real-Life Style Transformations: People Who Defied Adaptive Fashion Myths

These inspiring individuals prove that adaptive fashion isn't about compromise—it's about creativity, confidence, and breaking barriers!

- Case Study 1: Rhea's Saree Reinvention
- Challenge: Rhea, a 32-year-old lawyer, loved wearing sarees but found draping them difficult due to a spinal injury.
- Myth: "Sarees are too complicated for adaptive wear."
- **Transformation: She started using pre-stitched sarees with a built-in petticoat and magnetic pleats.**
- Style Impact: She now rocks her signature power look in court without needing assistance!
- Case Study 2: Vikram's Wedding Sherwani Upgrade
- Challenge: Vikram, 38, was getting married but struggled with traditional sherwanis that had too many buttons.
- Myth: "Sherwanis can't be adapted without losing their elegance."
- Transformation: His designer added hidden Velcro fastenings inside the sherwani, keeping the royal look intact.
- Style Impact: He looked regal on his wedding day while dressing up independently!
- Case Study 3: Tanya's Adaptive Street Style
- Challenge: Tanya, a 19-year-old college student with limited hand mobility, found zippers and buttons frustrating.

- Myth: "Adaptive fashion can't be trendy for young people."

- Transformation: She replaced all her hoodies and jackets with zip-up magnetic fastenings and swapped sneakers for no-lace slip-ons.

- Style Impact: Tanya now mixes oversized tees, statement sneakers, and magnetic denim—proving adaptive fashion can be street-style cool!

- Case Study 4: Raj's Wheelchair-Friendly Formal Wear

- Challenge: Raj, 45, an entrepreneur who uses a wheelchair, found that regular suits were uncomfortable when seated for long hours.

- Myth: "Formal wear isn't practical for wheelchair users."

- Transformation: He got custom-tailored suits with a high-back, short-front design and stretch panels for better movement.

- Style Impact: Raj now attends business meetings in sleek, adaptive suits that let him feel confident and comfortable.

- Final Takeaway:

These real-life stories prove that adaptive fashion is not about limits—it's about making clothes work for YOU. Whether it's a wedding, college, work, or casual wear, adaptive style can be effortless, elegant, and trend-setting!

17.7 Celebrity – Inspired Adaptive Outfit Ideas for Every Occasion

You don't need a red carpet to dress like a star! Here's how to recreate celebrity-inspired outfits with adaptive modifications for different events—keeping it stylish, comfortable, and hassle-free.

- Festive & Wedding Wear (Inspired by Deepika Padukone & Ranveer Singh)

- For Women:
  - Deepika's Classic Saree Look → Try a pre-stitched saree with magnetic pleats.
  - Heavy Lehengas? No Problem! → Opt for a lightweight lehenga with an elastic waistband & Velcro choli closure.
  - Dupatta Always Slipping? → Use clip-on dupatta fasteners to keep it secure.

- For Men:
  - Ranveer's Royal Sherwani Style → Swap buttons for hidden Velcro closures.
  - Dhotis Too Tricky? → Try an elastic, pre-stitched dhoti-pant.
  - Add a Statement Safa (Turban) → Use a pre-tied, clip-on version for easy styling.

- Final Touch: Pair with adaptive juttis with cushioned soles for all-day comfort.

- Work & Office Looks (Inspired by Priyanka Chopra & Ayushmann Khurrana)

- ⬚ For Women:
  - Priyanka's Sleek Power Dressing → Opt for a magnetic-front blazer & pull-on trousers.
  - Struggle with Tight Shirts? → Choose soft, stretch-fabric formal tops with hidden snaps.
  - Ditch the Heels! → Try adaptive block heels or stylish slip-on loafers.
- ⬚ For Men:
  - Ayushmann's Smart-Casual Suiting → Wear a stretchable Nehru jacket with easy Velcro buttons.
  - Trouble with Formal Shoes? → Switch to slip-on leather loafers with cushioned insoles.
  - No-Tie Shirts for Quick Dressing → Get pre-tied ties or zip-up mandarin-collar shirts.
- ⬚ Final Touch: Keep accessories minimal—a magnetic watch & easy-wear belt complete the look.
- ⬚ Party & Evening Outfits (Inspired by Sonam Kapoor & Shahid Kapoor)
- ⬚ For Women:
  - Sonam's Statement Fusion Wear → Try a front-zip jumpsuit with stretchable fabric.
  - Struggle with Tight Gowns? → Choose a wrap-style evening dress with hidden Velcro closures.
  - Chunky Jewelry Too Heavy? → Wear lightweight magnetic earrings & bracelets instead.

- ❐ For Men:

  - Shahid's Minimalist Black-Tie Look → Opt for a tuxedo with a side-zip closure for ease.

  - Leather Shoes Too Stiff? → Adaptive soft-sole dress shoes with arch support work just as well.

  - Jackets That Move With You → Get stretch-panel blazers for extra comfort.

- ❐ Final Touch: A stylish crossbody bag with an easy-access flap keeps essentials within reach.

- ❐ Travel & Vacation Outfits (Inspired by Alia Bhatt & Vicky Kaushal)

- ❐ For Women:

  - Alia's Breezy Travel Look → Go for a loose-fit, slip-on maxi dress with soft fabric.

  - Ditch the Backpack Struggles → Use a crossbody bag with a magnetic flap.

  - Adaptive Sneakers for Long Walks → Choose Velcro or step-in sneakers for no-lace convenience.

- ❐ For Men:

  - Vicky's Effortless Airport Style → Pull-on elastic cargo pants with an adaptive hoodie.

  - Shoes for Walking All Day? → Try stretchable, slip-on travel sneakers.

  - Lightweight Jackets That Fold Easily → Choose magnetic-closure jackets with hidden pockets.

🗐 Final Touch: Wear a bucket hat with an adjustable fit for sun protection.

🗐 Final Takeaway:

Dressing like a celebrity doesn't have to be complicated! With adaptive styling hacks, you can look effortlessly fashionable while keeping comfort & accessibility a priority.

17.8 Quick Celebrity – Inspired Outfit Hacks for Last-Minute Dressing

We all have those moments when we need to get ready fast but still want to look stylish and put together. Here are some quick, no-fuss celebrity-inspired outfit hacks that make dressing effortless, adaptive, and trendy.

🗐 Last-Minute Festive Outfit Hacks (Inspired by Kareena Kapoor & Hrithik Roshan)

🗐 For Women:

- Kareena's Classic Kurta-Churidar Look → Slip into a front-open kurta with pull-on leggings for instant elegance.

- Heavy Dupatta Drama? → Convert a dupatta into a cape by adding snap buttons to the shoulders—zero adjustments needed!

- Struggle with Bangles & Earrings? → Opt for cuff bracelets & magnetic clip-on earrings.

🗐 For Men:

- Hrithik's Effortless Ethnic Look → Swap traditional dhotis for pre-stitched drawstring dhoti pants.

- Can't Handle Sherwani Buttons? → Get a Velcro or zip-up Indo-Western jacket instead.

- Uncomfortable Mojaris? → Choose padded slip-on juttis or leather loafers.

- Super Quick Fix: Throw on a statement shawl or stole over a plain outfit—instant festive vibes!

- 5-Minute Workwear Hacks (Inspired by Anushka Sharma & Saif Ali Khan)

- For Women:

  - Anushka's Minimalist Chic Look → Pair a pull-on pencil skirt with a soft, side-zip blouse for effortless style.

  - Blazers Feel Restrictive? → Choose a stretch-fit blazer with open-front styling.

  - Too Tired for Heels? → Go for adaptive block-heel slip-ons—height without the struggle!

- For Men:

  - Saif's Clean-Cut Office Look → Try a button-free formal shirt with hidden snaps for easy dressing.

  - Ties Take Too Long? → Use a zip-up or clip-on tie—sharp and time-saving.

  - Belt Struggles? → Wear a stretchable, no-buckle belt for a polished look without effort.

- Super Quick Fix: Keep a structured jacket or shrug near the door—just throw it on to instantly elevate any outfit.

- Party & Date-Night Hacks (Inspired by Katrina Kaif & Ranbir Kapoor)

- For Women:

  - Katrina's Classic Black Dress Look → Go for a wrap-style dress with magnetic closures—easy to wear, flattering on all!

  - Struggle with Accessories? → Stick to one statement piece like a pre-layered necklace or magnetic bracelet.

  - Heels Too Much Work? → Swap stilettos for glamorous slip-on flats or platform sneakers.

- For Men:

  - Ranbir's Smart-Casual Charm → Pair adaptive stretch-fit jeans with a no-button Henley tee.

  - Jackets Are Too Stiff? → Try a zip-up bomber jacket with soft lining for comfort & style.

  - Shoes That Slip On Fast? → Go for elastic-laced sneakers or loafers—zero effort required!

- Super Quick Fix: Stick to monochrome outfits (all black, all white, etc.)—it always looks sleek and put together.

✈ Travel Outfit Hacks (Inspired by Alia Bhatt & Shah Rukh Khan)

- For Women:

- Alia's Airport-Ready Comfort → A loose-fit jumpsuit with a front zipper—effortless and stylish.

- Struggle with Big Bags? → Use a lightweight crossbody bag with easy magnetic closures.

- Can't Handle Shoe Changes? → Wear slip-on sneakers with memory foam soles.

For Men:

- SRK's Signature Travel Look → Stretch-fit joggers & a zip-up hoodie for comfort on the go.

- Backpacks Too Heavy? → Try a roll-top tote with Velcro straps for quick access.

- Cold Flight? → Keep a poncho or shawl with hidden pockets for a cozy, functional extra layer.

Super Quick Fix: If in doubt, throw on oversized sunglasses and a stylish jacket—instant celebrity airport vibes!

Final Takeaway:

Dressing like a celebrity doesn't have to be complicated! With these quick adaptive hacks, you can look put-together in minutes—without the struggle!

17.9 Emergency Wardrobe Fixes – Quick Hacks for Fashion Disasters

Fashion emergencies can happen anytime—whether it's a stubborn stain, a broken zipper, or an outfit that doesn't fit right. Here are some quick, adaptive hacks to save your look in minutes.

- ▢ Stain Removal Hacks – Fix It Before Anyone Notices!

  - Oil or Grease Stain?

- ▢ Fix: Sprinkle baby powder or cornstarch over the stain, let it absorb for 5 minutes, then brush off and dab with dish soap.

  - Coffee or Tea Spill?

- ▢ Fix: Dab the stain with a mix of vinegar and water—do NOT rub, as it will spread.

  - Makeup Smudges on Clothes?

- ▢ Fix: Use a bit of shaving foam to lift the stain without water.

  - Sweat Stains on Light Fabrics?

- ▢ Fix: Rub the area with a baking soda and lemon juice paste, then wash after 10 minutes.

- ▢ Clothing Damage – Quick Repairs Without Sewing

  - Broken Zipper?

- ▢ Fix: Rub pencil lead or a bar of soap over the stuck zipper to slide it back into place.

  - Button Fell Off & No Time to Sew?

- ▢ Fix: Use a paperclip or twist tie to loop through the hole and secure temporarily.

  - Hem Too Long & No Time to Tailor?

- Fix: Use double-sided tape or fabric glue for an instant hem fix.

  - Tight Sleeves or Pant Legs?

- Fix: Stretch the fabric gently with a warm steam iron or damp towel before wearing.

- Shoe Emergencies – Fix Uncomfortable or Broken Footwear

  - Shoes Too Tight?

- Fix: Wear thick socks and use a hairdryer on the tight spots to stretch them instantly.

  - Slippery Soles?

- Fix: Rub sandpaper or a potato (yes, really!) on the sole to add grip.

  - Heels Hurting Your Feet?

- Fix: Apply clear gel deodorant on pressure points to prevent blisters.

  - Straps Keep Falling?

- Fix: Attach a small piece of Velcro to keep them in place.

- Quick Fixes for Outfit Malfunctions

  - Dupatta or Scarf Keeps Slipping?

- Fix: Use clip-on fasteners or a magnetic brooch to secure it.

  - Bra Straps Showing Under Ethnic Wear?

- Fix: Use fashion tape to tuck them in place.

- Too Much Cleavage in a Low-Cut Top?

❐ Fix: Use a safety pin inside the fabric for an invisible fix.

- Fabric Too Itchy?

❐ Fix: Rub a dryer sheet over the clothing or spray lightly with hair conditioner & water mix.

❐ Final Takeaway:

Fashion emergencies don't have to ruin your day! With these quick hacks, you can fix any wardrobe disaster on the go—without stress!

Chapter 18

Dressing with Dignity – Confidence, Comfort & Self – Expression

Fashion is not just about clothes—it's about identity, confidence, and self-respect. For individuals with disabilities or mobility challenges, dressing up can feel like a daily battle, but it doesn't have to be. This chapter is about reclaiming control over personal style and making fashion work for YOU.

18.1 Dressing Should Be About Joy, Not Struggle

You deserve clothes that make you feel:

- Confident – Because you should never feel invisible.

- Comfortable – No more itchy seams, tight fits, or hard-to-fasten clothes.

- Independent (When Possible) – Adaptive fashion should make dressing easier, not harder.

🗇 Reminder: Your clothes should fit your body, not the other way around.

18.2 The Caregiver's Role – Making Dressing Easier & Respectful

If you assist someone with dressing, remember:

- Let them have a say – Even small choices like "blue or green?" help maintain dignity.

- Be patient & gentle – Avoid rushing; dressing should feel comfortable, not stressful.

- Choose clothes that promote ease – Look for side openings, soft fabrics, and adaptive fastenings to simplify the process.

Tip for Caregivers: If possible, lay out clothes in a step-by-step order to make dressing less overwhelming.

18.3 How to Feel Good in Your Clothes Again

Common Struggles:

"Fashion doesn't cater to my needs."

"I don't feel stylish anymore."

"Getting dressed takes too much effort."

Solutions:

- Modify your existing clothes – Small changes (Velcro instead of buttons, elastic waists) can make a big difference.

- Express yourself through accessories – Statement scarves, jewelry, and comfortable shoes can elevate any outfit.

- Find inspiration – Look at adaptive fashion influencers, brands, or real people who dress confidently despite challenges.

Reminder: You don't have to wear boring, plain clothes just because they're "functional." Style is personal—make it yours.

18.4 Dressing as Self-Love – Not Just a Necessity

Why should dressing up feel like a burden? Instead of thinking, "I have to wear something today," shift your mindset to:

- "I GET to wear something I love today."

- "I am dressing for ME, not for others."

- "My clothes reflect my personality, not my limitations."

🗖 Final Thought: The world may not always be adaptive, but your wardrobe can be. Wear what makes you feel seen, stylish, and celebrated.

🗖 Final Takeaway:

Dressing with dignity means:

- Feeling comfortable, stylish, and in control of your choices.

- Making fashion adapt to YOU—not the other way around.

- Embracing clothing as a form of self-respect and self-expression.

You deserve to feel good in what you wear—always.

Chapter 19

The Emotional Impact of Fashion – More Than Just Clothes

Clothing is deeply tied to self-esteem, identity, and even mental well-being. For individuals with disabilities or mobility challenges, the right fashion choices can mean more confidence, independence, and joy. This chapter explores the emotional side of dressing—how what we wear can shape how we feel.

19.1 Why Dressing Well Matters for Mental Health

We often underestimate how much fashion affects our mood. Clothing can be:

- A Confidence Booster – When you like how you look, you feel stronger and more self-assured.

- A Form of Self-Expression – Your outfit tells the world who you are before you even speak.

- A Mood Lifter – Bright colors, soft fabrics, and well-fitted clothes instantly improve energy levels.

Fact: Studies show that when people dress in clothes they feel good in, they perform better in daily activities, work, and social settings.

19.2 The Frustration of Limited Choices – And How to Overcome It

- Common Struggles:
- "Shopping is frustrating because nothing fits my needs."
- "I feel like I have to choose between comfort and style."
- "I don't feel represented in mainstream fashion."
- Ways to Take Back Control:
  - Customize your clothes – Small adaptive modifications make a huge difference.
  - Explore adaptive brands – More options are becoming available every year.
  - Get inspired – Follow adaptive fashion influencers or communities that celebrate inclusion.
- Mindset Shift: Instead of thinking, "Fashion isn't made for me," start thinking, "Fashion can be adapted to me."

19.3 How to Use Fashion as a Tool for Self-Empowerment

What if dressing wasn't just a task, but a daily act of self-care?

  - Experiment with Color Psychology –
- Blues & Greens → Calm and confident.
- Reds & Yellows → Energetic and bold.

🗗 Black & Neutrals → Classic and powerful.

- Create a Personal "Feel-Good" Outfit –

Have a go-to power outfit that makes you feel amazing every time you wear it.

- Dress for Yourself, Not Just Functionality –

Even if no one sees your outfit, you should love what you're wearing.

🗗 Reminder: Your clothes should empower you, not limit you.

19.4 Changing the Narrative – You Deserve Fashion That Works for YOU

The fashion industry may still be evolving, but you don't have to wait for brands to catch up.

- You can modify, adapt, and personalize your wardrobe to fit your needs.
- You deserve clothes that make you feel stylish, confident, and comfortable.
- Fashion is about self-expression—not limitations.

🗗 Final Thought: The next time you get dressed, don't just think about what's easiest—think about what makes you feel like YOU.

🗗 Final Takeaway:

Fashion isn't just about looking good—it's about feeling good. The right clothes can give you:

- More confidence in social settings.
- More comfort in daily life.

- More power in how you see yourself.

Wear what makes you feel unstoppable.

19.5 How Caregivers Can Help Boost Confidence Through Fashion

Caregivers play a vital role in helping individuals feel good about their appearance. Dressing isn't just a daily routine—it's an opportunity to uplift, empower, and restore dignity. Here's how caregivers can make fashion a positive experience rather than a frustrating one.

- Common Mistakes Caregivers Make (Without Realizing It)

- Rushing the dressing process – Makes the person feel like a burden.

- Choosing only "practical" clothing – Comfort matters, but so does style and personal expression.

- Ignoring preferences – Even small choices help someone feel more in control of their identity.

- Not considering ease of dressing – Struggling with buttons, tight fits, or rough fabrics can be avoided with adaptive options.

- Mindset Shift: Dressing isn't just about getting ready—it's about making someone feel seen, respected, and confident.

  - How Caregivers Can Make Dressing a Confidence-Boosting Experience

- Involve Them in Outfit Selection

- Let them pick colors, accessories, or fabrics—
  even small choices matter.

- Ask, "Do you feel good in this?" instead of
  assuming what's best.

⬚ Why It Works: Having control over their clothing restores dignity and independence.

⬚ **Choose Adaptive Fashion That Feels Like Regular Clothing**

- Look for Velcro, magnetic, or stretch fabric alternatives that don't look "medical."

- Find stylish options in mainstream brands— adaptive doesn't have to mean "different."

⬚ Why It Works: Feeling "normal" in fashion boosts self-esteem.

⬚ **Make Dressing a Stress-Free, Positive Ritual**

- Lay out clothes in a step-by-step order to reduce decision fatigue.

- Allow extra time for dressing—rushing can cause stress.

- Use mirrors to let them see themselves—visual affirmation builds confidence.

⬚ Why It Works: A relaxed dressing routine can start the day on a positive note.

⬚ Compliment Their Look!

- A simple, "You look great today!" can change how someone feels.

- Point out specific things ("This color suits you!" or "You always rock this style!").

🗇 Why It Works: People internalize how others see them—uplift, don't overlook.

🗇 Final Takeaway:

Caregivers have the power to turn dressing into an act of self-confidence rather than a daily chore.

- Encourage personal expression.

- Choose adaptive clothing that's stylish, not just functional.

- Make dressing a positive, stress-free experience.

🗇 Because everyone deserves to feel good in what they wear.

Chapter 20

Real Stories – The People Behind Adaptive Fashion

Fashion is deeply personal. It's more than just clothes—it's about self-expression, confidence, and dignity.
In this chapter, we share real stories of individuals, caregivers, and designers who have embraced adaptive fashion and transformed the way they dress.

20.1 Riya's Story – Rediscovering Style After a Spinal Injury

Riya, a 27-year-old marketing professional, was always a fashion enthusiast. But after a spinal injury left her in a wheelchair, dressing up became frustrating.

- Her Struggles:

- Traditional sarees felt impossible to drape.

- Formal wear often had zippers and buttons at the back, making dressing difficult.

- Shopping was discouraging because adaptive fashion wasn't widely available.

- Her Solution:

  - She started customizing her sarees with pre-stitched pleats and side zippers.

  - She switched to stretch-fit blazers and elastic-waist trousers for work.

- She found a local tailor willing to modify her favorite outfits into adaptive designs.

- Her Words: "I thought I had to give up on fashion, but instead, I just found a new way to make it work for me!"

20.2 Caregiver's Perspective – Dressing with Patience & Respect

Vikas, 45, takes care of his mother, who has Parkinson's disease. Dressing became a stressful process—buttons were hard, sleeves were tight, and she often felt helpless.

- What Wasn't Working:

- He used to pick only loose, easy clothes, but his mother felt like she was losing her sense of style.

- Morning routines became rushed, making dressing feel like a task instead of an experience.

- What Changed:

  - He started letting her choose her outfits, even if it took a little longer.

  - He replaced buttons with snap closures and added Velcro fastenings to her daily wear.

  - He took her shopping for adaptive clothing instead of assuming what she needed.

- His Words: "Adaptive fashion isn't just about clothing—it's about giving dignity back to the people we love."

20.3 The Tailor Who Became a Disability Fashion Expert

Meena, a local tailor in Mumbai, had never heard of adaptive fashion until one of her clients, a young woman with cerebral palsy, asked her to modify a lehenga.

🗇 Her Initial Challenge:

🗇 She had no training in adaptive modifications.

🗇 She didn't know how to replace zippers and buttons without ruining the design.

🗇 She assumed adaptive fashion had to be simple and plain.

🗇 How She Learned:

- She researched Velcro fastenings, side-open lehengas, and pre-stitched pleats.

- She started offering custom adaptive tailoring for elderly and disabled clients.

- She realized fashion should be for everyone—without limitations.

🗇 Her Words: "Before, I only made clothes. Now, I create confidence."

Chapter 21

Breaking Barriers – The Social Acceptance of Adaptive Fashion

Even as adaptive fashion grows, many people still don't see it as mainstream. This chapter explores why inclusive fashion should be normalized and celebrated.

21.1 Why Adaptive Fashion is Often Overlooked

- Common Social Attitudes:
- Many brands believe adaptive clothing is "niche" and not worth investing in.
- Fashion weeks rarely feature models with disabilities.
- Some people think adaptive wear looks "medical" instead of stylish.
- What Needs to Change?
  - Better representation in fashion magazines, films, and runways.
  - Major brands adopting adaptive fashion lines, not just niche startups.
  - Public awareness campaigns to make adaptive fashion mainstream.

21.2 Cultural Challenges in Adaptive Fashion

- In India, traditional clothing is deeply linked to identity, but most designs are not adaptive.

- People with disabilities often feel pressured to wear plain, easy outfits rather than what they love.

- Many elders accept discomfort because they don't want to trouble tailors for modifications.

- Solution: Make adaptive versions of regional wear available! Sarees, sherwanis, and salwar suits can all be modified without losing their beauty.

Chapter 22

Your Guide to Shopping for Adaptive Fashion in India

Finding adaptive clothing in India can be challenging, but it's getting easier! Here's how to shop smart and find the best options.

22.1 Where to Buy Adaptive Fashion in India

- Online Stores:

- Myntra Adaptive Section

- Amazon India (Search for "Velcro kurtas" or "elastic waist sarees")

- Urbanic & Ajio (For stretchable clothing)

- Tailors & Custom Designers:

- Many local tailors can modify existing outfits—you just need to ask!

- High-end designers like Sabyasachi & Tarun Tahiliani have started experimenting with pre-stitched, easy-drape outfits.

- NGOs & Adaptive Fashion Startups:

- Ability People (Hyderabad-based adaptive clothing brand)

- NGOs working on employment for disabled tailors

- Tip: Look for maternity fashion! Many maternity brands unknowingly create great adaptive wear.

Chapter 23

The Future of Adaptive Fashion – What's Next?

Fashion should be for everyone, and the future of adaptive wear is exciting!

23.1 What's Coming in Adaptive Fashion?

- AI-Powered Custom Fit Clothing – Smart measurements for perfect fits without trials.

- 3D-Printed Adaptive Shoes – Lightweight, ultra-comfortable shoes made just for your feet.

- Self-Fastening Clothes – Motion sensor shirts that adjust their fit automatically.

🗇 Fashion is evolving—adaptive wear will soon be as common as any other style.

Final Words: Fashion Without Limits

This book isn't just about clothing—it's about empowerment. It's about making sure:

- No one feels left out of fashion.

- Dressing up is a joy, not a challenge.

- Everyone, regardless of ability, has clothing that makes them feel strong and stylish.

🗇 Final Thought: Adaptive fashion isn't just a trend—it's the future.

Fashion Beyond Limits – A Message to Every Reader

As we come to the end of this book, there's one thing to remember: fashion is not about fitting into a standard—it's about making the standard fit you.

This isn't just a book about adaptive fashion—it's about embracing yourself, your needs, and your unique sense of style with confidence.

24.1 Your Body, Your Style, Your Rules

- Forget what society says fashion "should" be.
- Wear what makes you feel like YOU.
  - If you need Velcro instead of buttons—that's your fashion.
  - If you prefer pre-stitched sarees—that's your elegance.
  - If you love streetwear that's easy to put on—that's your vibe.
- Final Thought: You are not dressing to please the world—you are dressing to celebrate yourself.

24.2 The Real Meaning of Adaptive Fashion

Adaptive fashion is not just for:

- "People with disabilities"

- "The elderly"

- "Medical needs"

It's for anyone who wants clothing to work for them, not against them.

- It's for the new mother who needs easy-access outfits.

- It's for the busy professional who wants quick, effortless dressing.

- It's for the fashion-lover who refuses to compromise on style.

- Final Thought: Adaptive fashion is for EVERYONE, because everyone deserves clothing that makes life easier.

24.3 Your Personal Style Revolution Starts Now

- Take charge of your wardrobe – Modify, customize, and adapt clothes to fit your needs.

- Stop accepting discomfort as "normal" – Fashion should be a joy, not a struggle.

- Spread awareness – The more people embrace adaptive wear, the more it becomes mainstream.

- Final Thought: Fashion should adapt to people, not the other way around.

24.4 A Challenge for You – Make Fashion Your Own!

Before you close this book, try these:

- Modify one item in your wardrobe to make it more adaptive.

- Find an outfit that makes you feel truly confident and wear it proudly.

- Start a conversation with friends, family, or social media about the importance of inclusive fashion.

🗗 Final Thought: You have the power to redefine fashion for yourself and for the world. Own it.

🗗 Final Words: Adaptive Fashion is Just Fashion

This isn't a "special category" of clothing. This is just fashion done right—for every body, every need, and every style.

🗗 You are stylish. You are seen. You are limitless.

Closing Note

Fashion is not just about clothes—it's about identity, confidence, and self-expression. Through this book, I hope you've discovered that style has no limits, and neither do you.

To those who have struggled to find clothing that fits their needs—you are not alone. The world of fashion is evolving, and your voice, your preferences, and your comfort matter. Whether you're dressing for function, fashion, or both, your style should always reflect who you are, not just what is available.

To caregivers and loved ones—your patience and care in making dressing a dignified, joyful experience is invaluable. Fashion is one of the simplest ways to restore confidence, and your role in this journey is just as important as the clothes themselves.

- To designers, brands, and innovators—the future of fashion is inclusive. It's time to break the norms, rethink functionality, and create clothing that adapts to people, not the other way around.

- Most importantly, to you, the reader—you are seen, you are stylish, and you are limitless. Fashion is yours to define. Go forward, wear what makes you feel strong, and own your style with pride.

Fashion is not just what you wear—it's how you wear it. And you wear it beautifully.

The Future of Adaptive Fashion

The fashion industry is evolving, but adaptive fashion still has a long way to go. The future holds:

- More mainstream brands embracing inclusivity.
- Smarter fabrics and AI-driven customization.
- Better accessibility in retail and online stores.
- Stronger representation in fashion shows and media.

This is just the beginning. The more we talk about adaptive fashion, the more we push for change. Together, we can make inclusive fashion the norm, not the exception.

Resources & Recommendations

🗇 Online Stores & Brands for Adaptive Fashion

International: Tommy Hilfiger Adaptive, Zappos Adaptive, Nike FlyEase

Indian Brands: Ability People (Hyderabad), Aara by Avantika (custom adaptive wear)

🗇 Tailoring & DIY Guides

Find local tailors willing to modify existing clothes.

Use online sewing tutorials for DIY adaptive modifications.

Look for fashion schools incorporating adaptive design.

🗇 Remember: If you don't find what you need—create it! Adaptive fashion is about innovation and making clothing work for you.

Final Words: Wear Your Confidence

"Fashion is not just about what you wear; it's about how you feel when you wear it."

Whether you're dressing for a special occasion, work, or everyday life, your clothes should never feel like a struggle. They should be a reflection of who you are—bold, beautiful, and limitless.

This book is not just a guide; it's an invitation to redefine fashion on your own terms. To experiment, to adapt, and most importantly, to own your style with confidence.

If this book has inspired you, I'd love to hear your thoughts! Your feedback, stories, and ideas can shape the future of adaptive fashion.

- Share your thoughts, adaptations, or styling journeys at: Ka.pable Instagram

Thank you for being a part of this movement. Let's make fashion truly inclusive—together.

With warmth & gratitude,

Kashvi khurana